The Curious Yards and Alleyways of Morpeth

Bridget Gubbins

with original illustrations by Victor Ambrus

Published by
Greater Morpeth Development Trust

**Greater Morpeth
Development Trust**

Regeneration of town & countryside

www.gmdt.net

Published by:
Greater Morpeth Development Trust
Carlisle Park Lodge
Castle Square
Morpeth
Northumberland
NE61 1YD

First published 2011

British Library Cataloguing in Publication Data
A catalogue reference for this book is available from the British Library.

ISBN 978-0-9568683-0-5

Printed in Great Britain by Martins the Printers Ltd, Sea View Works, Spittal, Berwick upon Tweed, TD15 1RS

Contents

Preface

Traditional and metric measurements
Location of Morpeth in the UK

Preface

"Why do you think those boundary lines are curved like that?" the lecturer asked my class, as he showed us an old map of Morpeth on an overhead slide. The map was from 1860. We could see the lines of the main streets, converging on the Market Place, and all the lesser streets of the town. I could even identify the yard in which I live. There was a long pause. Someone then tentatively suggested: "Could it be because of the ploughing?" She was right. I was amazed. How could I have lived in Morpeth for thirty four years, and not realised that the shape of the town was formed by plough teams?

That amazement has led to this study. I'm not spending much time on the better known features of Morpeth, such as the Clock Tower, the Chantry, the remains of the castle, or the oldest church of St Mary's on the south side of the town. It is about the yards and alleyways, behind the main streets of the historic town centre, where people lived, especially the poorer people.

It led me down some surprising routes, and I have many people to thank. But if I have to thank anyone in particular, it must be John Hodgson, who compiled A History of Morpeth in 1832. He wrote that he had "drawn together, and digested into some order, a mass of materials, which may be considered as a broad foundation for future historians of Morpeth to build upon." Indeed he did. I found I referred to it constantly, and I realise that others have done so too. At one point he apologises: "The Annals, I fear, will be considered as too minute, especially in the abstracts of the numerous deeds in the Town's Hutch." They are minute, but there they are for us to use, as likewise are the ancient charters of the de Merlays. What would we do without his work, and Frank Graham who re-published it in 1973, making it easily accessible to all?

We are very fortunate also that the nationally renowned artist Victor Ambrus agreed to do the illustrations, bringing together aspects of the town from times long ago, in such a striking and human way.

Old Bakehouse Yard, Morpeth, 2011.   Bridget Gubbins

Acknowledgements
Greater Morpeth Development Trust, Tamsin Lilley Heritage Officer,
management and advice
John Griffiths and Kim Bibby-Wilson, reading and historical advice
Keith Gilroy, Northumberland Archives, IT and advice
Alan Davison, photos and IT
Elizabeth Williams, Northumberland Conservation, County Hall, advice and photos

Traditional and metric measurements

Area

1 acre	=	22 yards x 220 yards	=	4840 square yards
	=	or 69.57 yards x 69.57 yards	=	4840 square yards
1 rood	=	5½ yards x 220 yards, or ¼ acre		
4 roods	=	1 acre		

Metric equivalent

1 acre	=	4046.86 square metres
1 acre	=	0.4047 hectare, or approximately 40% of a hectare
1 hectare	=	approximately 2½ acres

Length

1 mile	=	1760 yards
1 furlong	=	220 yards, or 1/8 mile
1 chain	=	22 yards, or 1/10 furlong
1 yard	=	3 feet

Metric equivalent

1 mile	=	1609.34 metres
1 yard	=	0.9144 metre
1 metre	=	1.0936 yards

"The market town of Morpeth lies on the River Wansbeck, a little to the east of the present A1, in an undulating and wooded landscape between rural foothills to the west and low-lying coastal plain to the east. Morpeth is one of Northumberland's larger towns with a population of around 14,500 and is also the county town and administrative base for the county council. It lies 13 miles north of Newcastle, a similar distance from Alnwick and 12 miles from the North Sea, extending over both north and south banks of the River Wansbeck where it takes a broad southward loop."

Finlayson, R, Hardie, C, et al, *Morpeth: Northumberland Extensive Urban Survey,* Northumberland County Council, 2009

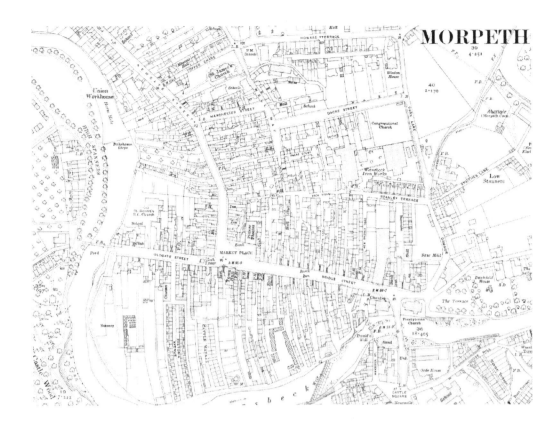

Above: OS map 1922 3rd edition
Below: Morpeth town centre, 1960s, Turners (Photography) Ltd, Newcastle upon Tyne

1   It all started with the ploughmen   1060 - 1160
The ancient traces of early Morpeth

Morpeth is founded on the work of the ploughmen. This story will reveal the hidden patterns which lie under the town centre, formed by the labouring ox teams and the humble villagers of the early middle ages. The alleyways which now cut through the buildings on the main streets have captured these ancient tracks. They are secretive and compelling in their own way, leading us through little yards, sometimes to another street, or sometimes to havens like the Old Bakehouse Millennium Green.

The story will take us from the earliest days of the Norman conquest to the present time. We will look at old maps, and create new maps to try to work out how it happened. We'll also think about the people who established the town, particularly the poorer people; from the ploughmen and their families to those who lived in the back yards of the middle ages; from the paupers in the crowded slums to residents of the present day.

To start us off, we can take a quick look on the frontispiece at a map from 1922 and compare it with an aerial photo from the 1950s. Both show the maze of yards and alleyways behind the main streets, which are Oldgate, Bridge Street and Newgate Street. In the enthusiastic rush of modernisation in the 1960s and 1970s, many of these buildings were pulled down. This would have been an easier story to write sixty years ago. Nevertheless, traces of the work of the ploughmen can still be seen, and I maintain that these ancient patterns are as important as any other historic boundaries in Northumberland, as the drove roads across the moorlands, as the mounds of buried lost medieval villages, or the ramparts of the prehistoric hillforts. Perhaps they are even more important, because we tread these routes as part of our everyday lives, as we go shopping, and as we take short cuts to the bus station or the park.

We cannot talk about the work of the poor ploughmen, or the paupers in the slums, without thinking about those who shaped their lives. The Norman barons and their descendants; the kings of England and Scotland who marched their troops along the routes through the fields; the later burgesses who controlled the trade in the town; the government inspector whose job it was to improve nineteenth century sanitation in the slums; the borough council in the twentieth century; they all have their parts to play.

As we look at the map and the aerial photo at the beginning of this chapter, we can see lines of buildings in curving rows. The north/south lines in the town centre are not totally straight. What could be the reason for this? If people wanted to mark out gardens or building plots, why wouldn't they just do it in straight lines? If they wanted curved plots, as might happen in a modern housing development, why wouldn't they make really curly curves?

The reason takes us back to the start of our story, almost a thousand years. It is hard to imagine what the landscape was like in 1000 AD, before the arrival of the Norman conquerors, and there is little or no documentary evidence of life here at that time.

We can conjecture however that our Anglian forebears were farming here, in the fertile land next to the river. There would have been woods on the surrounding hillsides. There was probably some common land, and perhaps a wooden church on the site of the existing parish church of St Mary the Virgin, on the hilly southern side of the town.

There must have been some simple village homesteads near the church, or in the low land in the loop of the Wansbeck, which is the area of this study, but no traces of them remain.

Most of us have studied the open field system of farming in school. Large fields were cultivated, communally, in strips, by peasants, the majority of whom were bondmen, tied by obligations of labour and often payment of goods to the local lord of the manor. Two of every three fields were farmed each year, leaving the third fallow. This form of farming was usual before the Norman conquest and until the Black Death around 1350. After this time, much land was enclosed, a process which peaked 18th and early 19th centuries, and which produced the fields and hedgerows with which we are familiar today.

The first Norman baron of Morpeth, William de Merlay, is believed to have established a wooden castle at Ha' Hill in about 1080.₁ After that, his son Ranulph de Merlay became the baron, and he initiated the setting up of the Abbey of Newminster in 1138. Ranulph's son Roger became Roger de Merlay l, and although we don't know much about what he did in Morpeth, he may have set up a few homesteads on the fields north of the river, as we will see later.

There are no maps dating from the twelfth century. (The most important later maps can be found in the appendices at the end.) Because what happened at that time underlies the later development of the town, I am going to try to create one, at a date of around 1160, during the time of Roger de Merlay l.

For this created map, Fig 1.1, I am using as a basis the 1852 plan of the borough of Morpeth by Hoggar and Rapier, surveyed for the Local Board of Health in 1852, which can be seen at Appendix 3 and also Fig 1.3.

Let us try to forget Newgate Street, Bridge Street and Oldgate. This was an area of agricultural strip farming, villagers using oxen to plough the fields for cereal crops. They would have also needed meadows to provide hay for winter food for the animals, which would be near the River Wansbeck and the burns. Woodlands and commons would have been on the outer fringes.

On my created map, I've traced the outlines of ploughed strips of land, basing them on what can still be seen on the 1852 map, and showing the direction in which they lay. A sizeable block of strips runs north/south from Oldgate, and may have run across it. For convenience, I'm calling that the Oldgate block. A huge block runs north/south across where Bridge Street is now. I'm calling that the Bridge Street block.

North of that is a large west/east block stretching down from the bank of the Wansbeck, and sloping gradually towards the Cottingburn. I'm calling this the Newgate South block.

North again is a block of short strips on both sides of the Cottingburn. It is possible that these short strips were not ploughed. I'm calling this the Newgate North block.

These four blocks show most clearly the ancient patterns which were still apparent when the 1852 map was surveyed. We will look at them, and the other blocks, in detail, to see if my created map can be confirmed by other evidence, as the way this land might have been farmed in the open field system, as long ago as 1160.

The reasons for creating my map will become clearer as we proceed. I have grouped them into sections.

- **First,** the pattern of the later yards and alleyways of Morpeth gives us many clues.

- **Second**, we can compare the lengths and widths of strips used in medieval open field farming, and see if they relate to the patterns in Morpeth.

- **Third**, the landforms land dictate how the strips would be laid out.

- **Fourth**, some evidence is available from place names.

First, the pattern of the yards and alleyways of Morpeth
The 1852 map, Fig 1.3, shows a layout of strips along the Oldgate, Bridge Street and Newgate South blocks which are slim, long, and slightly curved. The frontispiece map and photo show the same characteristics. The strips appear roughly similar in width, though the length varies according to the route of the River Wansbeck.

The slight backward curve indicates an ancient field system. It is an important characteristic, often referred to by historians as a flattened reverse-S shape. It has been captured in Morpeth. How did it happen? The answer is that this is the way the ox teams ploughed the strips.

As the ploughshare cut the furrow, the mouldboard behind turned the furrow-slice to the right. As the oxen reached the end of the furrow, the ploughman turned them to the left, until they were lined up along the unploughed headland, facing left. They were then turned around to the right, and lined up ready to start the next furrow, so that they were ploughing in a clockwise direction, as shown in Fig 1.2. Ploughing was a task requiring great skill and experience, and there are good reasons for doing it in this way. It avoided cutting across the furrows that were already ploughed. It allowed a wider turn for the oxen.[2]

Another benefit of the gentle curve to the left is that the headland area required to turn the plough could be narrower, if the turn was made at an obtuse angle.[3]

The curved shape of the strips, side by side, makes sense. Once the first were established, adjoining strips followed the pattern. Skilled ploughmen would produce precise parallel furrows. If they did not, wasteful and unsightly patches of land would appear between groups of strips as they came together.

Thus, despite the centuries of changes that have taken place since the ploughmen worked the land, the patterns they established can be identified on nineteenth century and later maps, and on photos taken in recent times.

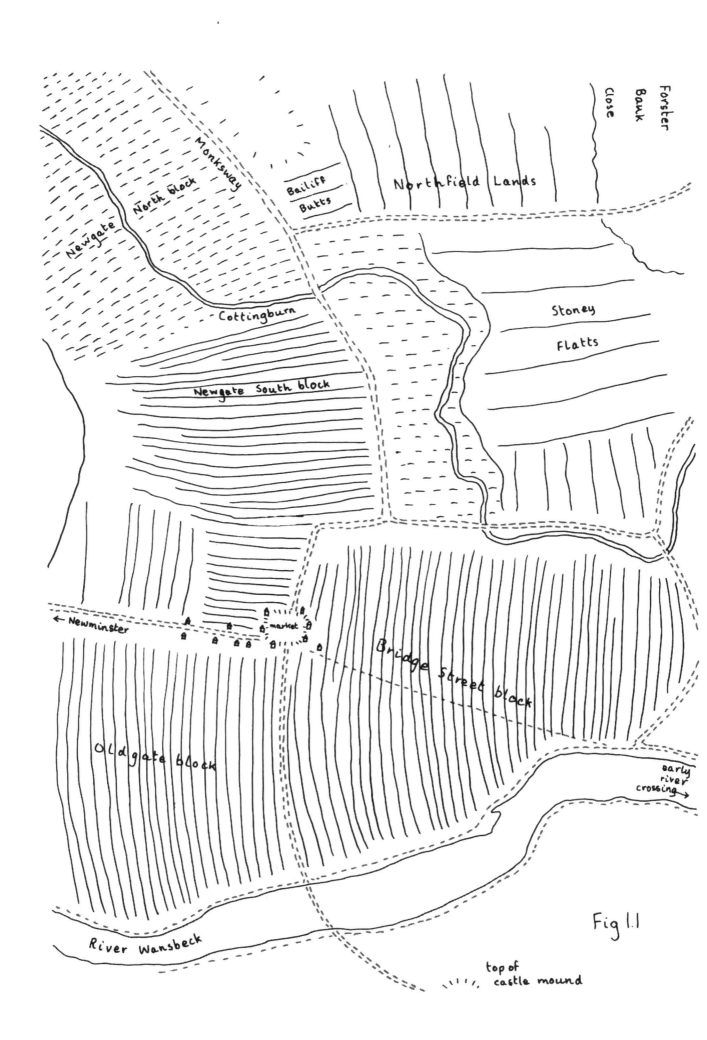

Forster
Bauk
Close

Monksway

North block

Newgate

Bailiff
Butts

Northfield Lands

—Cottingburn

Stoney

Flatts

Newgate South block

← Newminster

market

Bridge Street block

Oldgate block

early
river
crossing

Fig 1.1

River Wansbeck

top of
castle mound

4

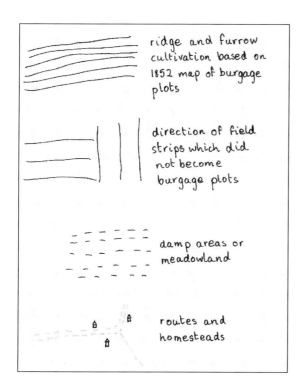

ridge and furrow cultivation based on 1852 map of burgage plots

direction of field strips which did not become burgage plots

damp areas or meadowland

routes and homesteads

Fig 1.1   Suggested map of Morpeth 1160 AD, showing the open field system, based on 1852 plan of the borough of Morpeth
Scale 1:2640, 24 inches to the mile

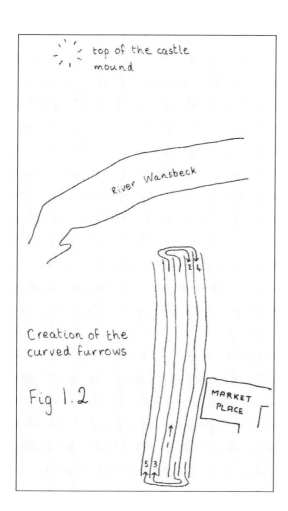

top of the castle mound

River Wansbeck

Creation of the curved furrows

Fig 1.2

MARKET PLACE

Fig 1.2

The ox teams created the curved rigs by pulling to the left at the end of the furrows, and then turning round to the right to plough the adjoining furrow.

On this pattern, established by the twelfth century, much of the new town of Morpeth was laid out.

The width of the furrows is exaggerated. The location is roughly where the Turk's Head, King's Head and Queen's Head yards are now.

Second, the lengths and widths of the strips

I wanted to see if these patterns were typical of medieval strips, so I had to get to grips with some almost obsolete measurements. Here, we'll see that those ploughed furrows relate to the history of the yards and alleyways of Morpeth in a direct way.

I am old enough to remember having to learn in school that there were 1,760 yards to a mile, and eight furlongs to a mile, not to mention 22 yards to a chain and 220 yards to a furlong. For this study, I also had to think about acres, and roods, the fractions into which they were broken down. The nineteenth century maps of Morpeth used these measurements. (See the measurements table earlier.)

A theoretical typical acre is 220 yards long, and 22 yards wide. In other words, it is a furlong in length. It is a chain in width. A furlong's original meaning is a *furrow long*. The acre strips would be 220 yards by 22 yards, which equals 4840 square yards. (Furlongs are sometimes used as measurements of area, but I am only using them in this study as lengths.)

I produced a model of an acre strip at the scale of the 1852 map, 1: 2640, and have laid it on the map, Fig 1.3. If the map is produced without reduction, the measurements of the strip at the correct scale are 3/10 inch by 3 inches.

You can move it around in your imagination, and apply it to the map. It relates very well to lengths of the strips in the Oldgate, Bridge Street and Newgate South blocks. It also relates well to the Stoney Flatts block and the strips in the North Field, and if it is imagined at half the scale lengthwise, you can check it on maps 2 – 6 in the appendix.

This is not to claim that the strips were an exact furlong in length. The difficulty of the land being ploughed, and the land formation, would always determine their length, so they could be longer or shorter. Also, there would be a *headland* of about 5 yards at each end for turning. Nevertheless, the model acre matches pretty well in Morpeth. These were typical medieval field strips.

Fig 1.3
The 1852 Local Board of Health plan of the Borough of Morpeth, with a one acre strip towards the east end of Bridge Street.
Courtesy of the Society of Antiquaries of Newcastle upon Tyne.

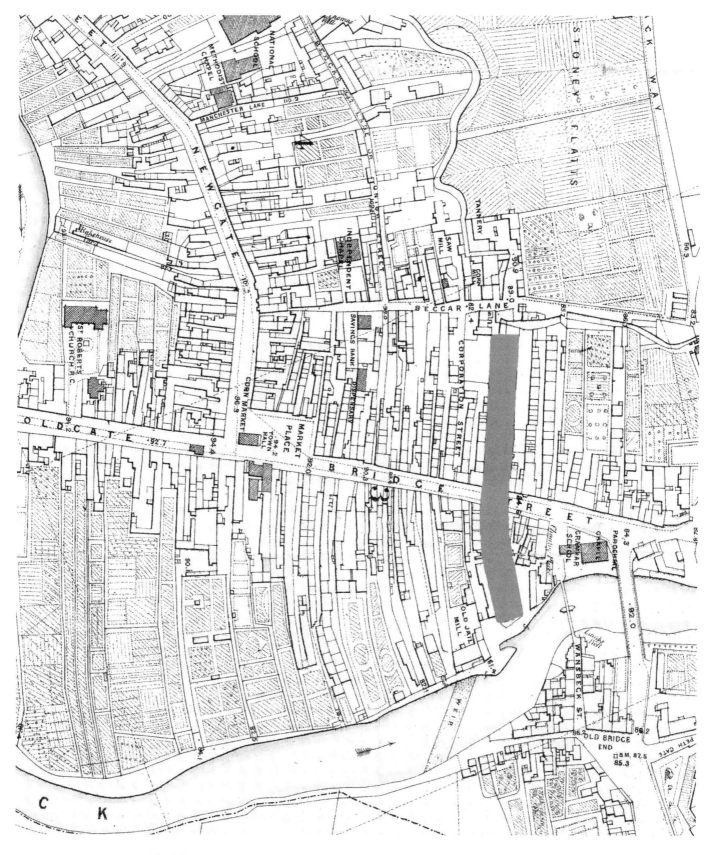

Fig 1.3

I have learned in the process of thinking about all this that an acre has a meaning. It is not just an arbitrary area of land devised for no particular reason. Theoretically, it has been described as the amount of land a plough team could work in a day, but it would vary according to the ease or difficulty of the land. There are studies which show that a day's ploughing varied between 2/3 and 3/4 of an acre.[4]

This acre strip in the medieval system consisted of many ploughed furrows. The furrows were built up into ridges by the ploughmen, and most of us are familiar with fields showing ridge and furrow in Northumberland. How many ridges were there in a 22 yard wide strip? This might seem an annoying and irrelevant question, but in fact it is significant. It relates to present day boundaries in the historic centre of Morpeth, as we'll see shortly.

The width of a ridge was usually at least five metres, or five and half yards, wide[5]. If we step out ridges which we find in Northumberland's fields, this will often be the case. Sometimes they are more, or sometimes less, but five-and-a-bit yards is a commonly found width. We can find it in the field known as The Mellows, on our right as we walk up to Lancaster Park, on the edge of Morpeth.

An acre would then consist of four ridges, each a little more than five yards wide, and about 220 yards long, and this is the model I've created at the correct scale of the map, Fig 1.3.

So far, we have now learned that the ploughmen's methods produced long strips, about four to the acre. Many were curved, and formed in a corrugated ridge and furrow pattern.

Third, the landforms dictate how the strips were laid out
In order to interpret further the pattern of the strips in my created map, based on the 1852 map, we need to think about the landforms. The medieval ploughmen knew very well what they were doing. They laid out the strips so that water would drain out between the furrows, usually in a downhill direction, towards a watercourse. Depending on how the land lies, after going so far in one direction, they would need to create a set of strips in another direction, often at right angles.

The Bridge Street and Oldgate blocks slope slightly downhill towards the River Wansbeck. They have a well-defined north/south alignment, the strips shortening towards the east.

The strips in the Newgate South block run in a west/east direction, from the higher bank of the Wansbeck towards the Cottingburn, though they may have stopped before the damper area near the stream.

I did not mark the Newgate North block with ploughed strips. This is a long narrow area, between the high bank of the Wansbeck to the west, and over the Cottingburn as far as the track Monksway. It is unlikely that the plough teams would have ploughed down this steep bank, crossed the stream and continued up the steep bank on the other side. They may have ploughed short strips, or there may be a different explanation. The open field system needed hay for winter food for the animals, and this was produced on damp meadows which were usually near watercourses. In Laxton, in Nottinghamshire, where an open field farming is still practised, the long strips of land bordering the streams are used in this way. There would still have been theoretical divisions, the villagers each knowing their own *dole,* or portion.

Another probable meadow area is on the banks of the Cottingburn, between the Stoney Flatts and the Newgate South block. The 1852 map shows an area of likely flooding here. The flat area where Low Stanners is now could well have been meadow too, as it was subject to regular flooding.

Finally, the North Field area is a slope leading down a steep bank, flattening towards what is now Howard Road and Howard Terrace. Here the strips would probably have run in a natural north/south direction. The present day street boundaries have a north/south tendency.

Fourth, evidence from place names
From old maps of Morpeth, the first dating from 1604, and the nineteenth century maps from 1826, 1852 and 1860, all of which can be found in the appendix section at the end, I have been able to track down a few names which have survived to this day, which help to affirm the existence of the open field farming in Morpeth.

Let us look at the North Field first. On the maps of 1604, 1826 and 1852, it is called North Field. In 1860, the first edition Ordnance Survey, it is called Northfield Lands. *Lands* is another name for *strips*.[6] Thus, the Northfield Lands may well have been the original strips.

The name Northlands still survives, in the road which leads beyond Thorpe Avenue, and in the care home on Kings Avenue. Both are situated on the former Northfield Lands.

Why do we only see North Field, if this area was part of an open field system? There were frequently three huge fields, often named as South Field, West Field, East Field or North Field.

On the 1604 map, there is no South Field, West Field or East field, except for those associated with Newminster Abbey which was a different system. We do find however East Parke, 418 acres, and West Parke, 142 acres. It is possible that what were once cultivated strips in an East Field and West Field had become pasture by 1604, thus the changed name. Also it is possible that the North Field, marked as composing 72 acres on this map, ranged over all of the low area towards the Wansbeck, including all the blocks which I have outlined.

In the North Field block, there are three more clues. Forster (or Foster) Baulk Close is a field named on the 1826 and 1852 maps. In the open field farming system, *baulks* separated groups of strips, and were not ploughed. They sometimes acted as access routes. Sometimes there was a change of level there, or there was a stream requiring a break in the closely ploughed strips. There is a burn flowing down the North Field to this day. It appears on the Ordnance Survey 1860 map, running between the Forster Baulk fields and Lady Close, acting as a boundary. The name *baulk* thus adds to the evidence that here was one of the great open fields.

Another tiny clue appears in the 1852 map, in the south west corner of North Field, and that is the wording Bailiffs Butts. The way strips were laid out on the landscape meant that, at times, little odd bits were left over. These were called *butts*. They could be cultivated, even though they were short. We find the word used to this day, in modern ploughing competitions, where *ploughing the butts* is a special skill. The word *butts* however is also used for archery targets, so this evidence is a little less certain.

Another of the large blocks of strips on my created map is at Stoney Flatts. This land is the area in the loop of the Cottingburn, as it flows south, east and then north to the River Wansbeck. The name *flatt* is another historic relic which means a group of strips. The name

Stoney Flatts is found on the 1852 map, where we can see suggestions of the direction in which the strips ran. Thus here is another trace of the former open field system.

Fig 1.4

Morpeth place name elements

baulk	OE balca, unploughed division between units of land
butt	ME butte, shorter strip of land
	ME butt, mound for archery practice
flatt	ME divisions of the common field
furlong	OE furlang, originally a furrow length
gate	ON gata a road
haugh	OE halh, alluvial land in a river bed
land	OE a strip of ploughland in the common field
ridge,rig,rigg	OE hyrcg, strip of land in an open field
rood	OE rod, about ¼ acre
yard	OE geard, land by a building, enclosure, rod in length

From Stan Beckensall's Place Names and Field Names of Northumberland, pp83-86 and 158

ber	OE bere, barley (Cameron, p213)
burgess/burgage	OF burgeis, person who lived in a town,
	occupier of a burgage, a property on which rent was payable (various)
how	ON hill, mound, tumulus (Cameron p227)
toft	OD toft, homestead, site of house and outbuildings (Cameron, p219)

OE old English. ME middle English. OF old French. ON old Norse. OD old Danish.

One final remnant of place name evidence is not from maps, but from our own living memory. Most Morpeth people use the term Back Riggs for the area around the bus station, but it no longer exists as a Morpeth address. My postman Brian Hedley informs me that the last postal address which used the name was the Inland Revenue, at 5 Back Riggs. This address ceased with the new Sanderson Arcade redevelopment completed in November 2009. *Riggs* means the same as ridges, and the name refers to the ridges and furrows of the medieval past. The name is a curious relic of long ago, as it must have been many hundred of years since strip farming actually occurred on that site. Now that there is no postal address, this place name will become lost in everyday memory, like Stoney Flatts, unless we make a special effort to commemorate it.

Maps and photographs, measurements, the way the land lies, and place names; that is quite a lot of evidence about how the land looked before the town existed, and upon which its later shape was formed.

My created map also shows some routes through the fields, to significant locations. At this time, there was probably a rudimentary market, although certain knowledge of it comes with the market charter of 1199. Ways would be formed to the market from the most important directions, from the castle, the abbey, and outlying settlements through the farmed strips.

There would have been one or more river crossings between the castle and the Market Place. The Wansbeck would have been fordable in several locations before the building of weirs, especially in summer. One was possibly downstream from where the Telford Bridge is now, where the stones of a ford have been seen in living memory. This crossing would be where the principal north/south route crossed the Wansbeck. There are suggestions that a wooden bridge was built here, in about 1250[7], before the construction of the medieval stone bridge which is now the footbridge. It is possible that the route continued upstream along the north bank of the River Wansbeck, running up between some strips towards the market, or it may have cut through them at an angle.

Another crossing could well have been between the castle and the market, along the south bank of the River Wansbeck, somewhere near where the Elliot Bridge is now. The 1826 map shows a footpath running along the river bank here.

A route would almost certainly have led from the Market Place to Newminster Abbey, which was established in 1138. It would have forded the river at the western end of the street which became Oldgate. There was a ford here until the twentieth century, and stepping stones are shown on the 1826 map.

Other routes would have approached the market from the east. One may have followed the Wansbeck along the path we still use by Tommy's Field, making its way between the strips of the Stoney Flatt block and Bridge Street block, before turning south into the Market Place. Another could have come in along what is now Howard Terrace, between the North Field and the Stoney Flatts, before turning south.

Another route would have led north from the Market Place. It is likely that an earlier route north followed what is now Cottingwood Lane. Hodgson translates it from one of the de Merlay charters as Monksway (Fig 2.2).[8] Perhaps it was used by the monks from the abbey, who then turned left along the old pathway now called Beggar's Lane, before dropping down to the Wansbeck on their way to Newminster. This path is just a little too far to the north to be seen on maps 2 to 6 in the appendices.

Finally, although we don't know any locations, by 1160, a few homesteads may have been established here and there, perhaps on some of the strips of land near the market, in the Oldgate block area, which from its name suggests is the oldest part of town.

All this is speculative, and yet the combined evidence gives us a picture of how it may have been. It is fascinating to imagine Morpeth as a medieval open field, to picture the ploughmen coaxing the lumbering oxen along the furrows, making their way home to their hovels of mud and straw and timber at the end of the long day; or in the autumn, the women gleaning with the children what they could find in the lord's demesne after the harvest, grinding the grain into a rough flour for their bread. This situation however was due to change. Next, we'll encounter the de Merlay barons, with their power and their ideas, their domination and development, which would alter the town for ever.

Ploughing in the shadow of the de Merlay castle, 1160

2   Houses on furrows   1160 - 1260
      The de Merlay barons lay out the new town of Morpeth

William the Conqueror's supporters were rewarded with the lands of England. By about 1080, they had control of Northumberland, and William de Merlay became baron of Morpeth.

They were the strong, dominant conquerors, speaking their alien French language, and they built their first wooden castle on the hill overlooking the river. The land was theirs, and the native inhabitants had to work it for their benefit.

Over the course of the next hundred and fifty years, the barons built a town on the agricultural land. They did it by granting charters. The word *granting* embodies a feeling of kindness, *noblesse oblige*, doing good things for the underlings as a favour. However, it was nothing like this. It was a business investment, and they needed wealth.

John Hodgson wrote his history of Morpeth in 1832, and I have used it extensively in what follows. He includes all the ancient documents to which he had access at that time, as well as charters in their Latin versions and his summaries of them in English.

Let's take over from where we left the last map, in about 1160. This is the time of the de Merlays, barons of Morpeth.

Roger de Merlay l   Baron of Morpeth from an uncertain date to 1188
During the time in which he was baron, Roger de Merlay l began the first tentative foundation of the borough, around 1150. His grandfather William de Merlay had fought with William the Conqueror at the Battle of Hastings, and he had obtained Morpeth in about 1080. His father Ranulph established the Abbey of Newminster in 1138. We don't know when Roger took over his barony, but Hodgson records his death as being in 1188.[1]

These are hazy, long ago days, with little definite information. Roger would have lived in his castle, the earlier wooden castle on Ha' Hill, south of the river. There may have been a simple church on the site of the medieval St Mary the Virgin, and some village houses between the castle and the church. We don't know if there were any houses in the land north of the Wansbeck, but there would have been cultivation.

Like all the Norman barons, he would have wanted to maximise his returns from the land under his control, and have seen the opportunity to start a settlement. The only information we have about how he did that is taken from documents concerning his son, Roger de Merlay ll, which are described below. From them, we can deduce that Roger de Merlay l set up the early beginnings of a town, which may have had a market. The earliest part of the town was likely to be on what came to be called Oldgate, and this is what I've called the Oldgate block, in my first created map in chapter 1.

Roger de Merlay ll   Baron of Morpeth 1188 - 1239
Roger de Merlay ll inherited the barony after the death of his father in 1188.[2] In 1199, King John came to the throne. That same year, Roger de Merlay ll decided to strengthen his borough.

Hodgson reports: "In the year of good king John, he paid a fine of 20 marks, and 2 good palfreys, for the privilege of having a market and a fair in his manor of Morpeth."[3]

In the charter he gave to the borough, Roger de Merlay ll *confirmed* his father's grant. The translation in English is: "I give, grant, and by this charter confirm to my free burgesses of Morpathia, to them and their heirs, all liberties and free customs, to be holden and had of me and my heirs for ever, honourably, freely, and wholly, as the charter of our lord the king, which I have, sets forth."

The word *confirm* here is important. Upon it Hodgson bases the pre-existence of a borough. "Here are free burgesses at the time of the grant, and *confirmation* of the privileges which probably existed before."₄ (My italics.) He uses the term *burgesses,* which means townspeople, those who live in a borough.

Hodgson also records that Roger de Merlay II is said to have "embellished the borough of Morpeth," the implication again being that the borough already existed. The words *confirmation* and *embellished* are the clues which enable us to guess what Roger de Merlay l had already done.

As for *confirmation,* it was quite usual for barons to confirm the existence of charters. It was a kind of renewal process. The barons had to pay the sovereign for their charters, hence the 20 marks and two good palfreys (warhorses) paid by Roger de Merlay ll to King John. A new charter raised money for the sovereign's exchequer, and re-established confidence for the baron and the borough that the king accepted their rights.

The wording in the charter seems to suggest that the king gave Roger de Merlay ll a charter, and that the baron then gave another one to the borough.

This was a very restless period of history. Hodgson records that in 1216, "King John, in the beginning of this year, marched against his rebellious barons in the north; many of whom had offended his irritable genius by doing homage to the king of Scotland at Felton." He reports two contradictory sets of evidence about the burning and destruction of the castle by the king as he passed through Morpeth.₅ He also remarks: "King John, when he battered down its castle in 1215, is said to have burnt the town, and this might give to Roger de Merlay the Second, in whose time it happened, the opportunity of embellishing it, which an old tradition gives him the credit of doing."₆

By 1199, therefore, we know that there were some town properties and that there was a charter for a marketplace and fair. The location of the market is not certain, but likely to be situated where it is now,₇ on a slightly raised situation to take account of the likelihood of flooding. It is also possible that the boundaries of the properties which exist along Oldgate now, such as the Grey Bull Yard, Challoner Place and Pretoria Avenue, were established by 1199. The area around the immediate town would still have been mainly agricultural, with the bonded labourers ploughing and harvesting as they had always done.

Roger de Merlay lll   Baron of Morpeth 1239 - 1266
We can really get to grips with the development of the town as more detailed information emerges from the charters of Roger de Merlay lll, son of Roger de Merlay ll. He assumed the barony of Morpeth in 1239, on the death of his father. He had to pay £100 to King Henry lll for this privilege.₈ As usual, the sovereign wanted every source of income he could get, and in his turn, de Merlay would want the same.

At some time during the late 1200s, the bridge was built over the river in the situation of the current footbridge, and the Chantry beside it. Also at some uncertain date, the original wooden castle on Ha' Hill was abandoned, and the new one built of stone, a little to the south.

It may have been after King John had quelled the barons and crushed the town in 1216.[9]
Town development with its associated costs was taking place.

Hodgson examined Morpeth's annals, which are the annual records, in the Town Hutch of
Morpeth, in 1832, and much of the following information is taken from them. He described
the three charters of Roger de Merlay lll, and reproduced the original Latin versions. A
selection from his book can be seen in Fig 2.2.[10] Roger de Merlay lll was the baron who
greatly enlarged the borough, and granted the tofts upon which the later pattern of Morpeth,
with its future yards and alleyways, evolved.

There were three charters. The first is that in which Roger de Merlay lll confirmed his father's
grant, in, or shortly after, 1239. He added various details about the rights of the burgesses,
and to the use of his corn fields, meadows and stubbles. He also granted pasture rights on his
wheat stubbles from Wincher-le-Way as far as the land of the abbot of Newminster, and the
dyke of the West Park, but not for the first fifteen days after harvest.

The second and third charters are the ones in which he granted land, and most relevant here.
From them, I have produced my second created map, Fig 2.1, showing as well as I was able
the location of the new grants to the borough. After the closest study of the wording of the
charters, and all the map evidence that is available, as well as considering the layout of the
land and position of the Cottingburn, some of the locations seem likely whereas others are
difficult to affirm. Nevertheless, I have made an attempt, because the evidence, such as it is,
is just too tempting.

So let's look at my second created map, based on the second and third charters, and on the
assumption that the baron's intention was to build town properties on the tofts described in the
charters. A *toft* is an enclosure of land for a homestead.[11] I am bearing in mind that Roger de
Merlay lll probably decided to construct wide routes along where Bridge Street and Newgate
Street are now, through the existing strips. Also we don't know for sure if the bridge and the
mill at their current location were yet built, although it is possible that these developments
were related. The date is 1239.

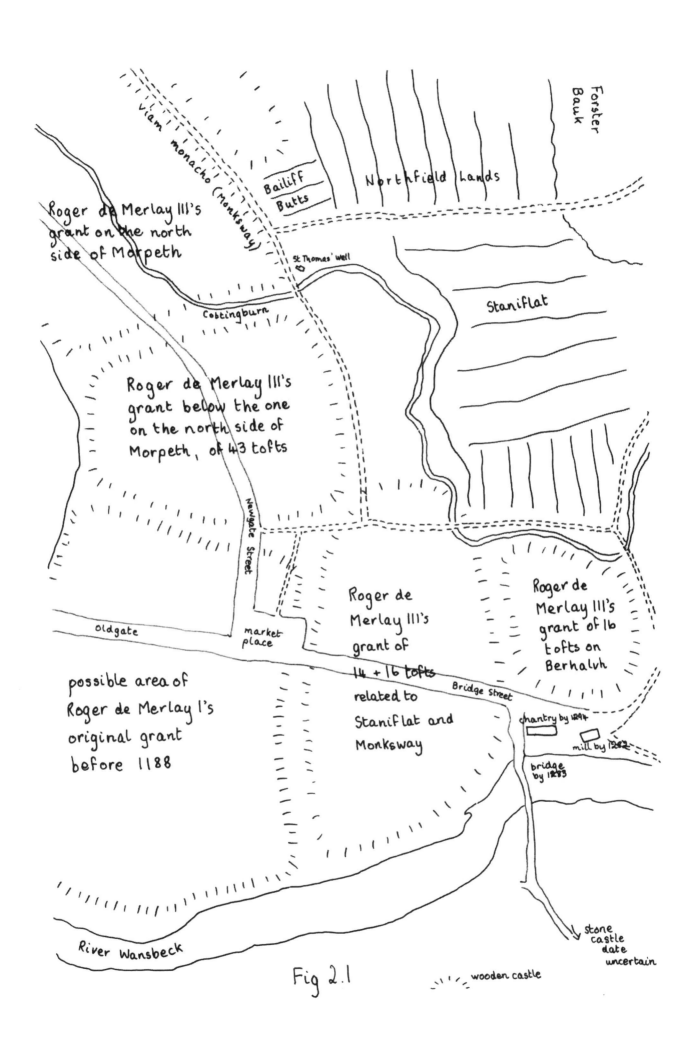

Forster Bauk

Northfield Lands

Bailiff Butts

viam monacho (Monksway)

Roger de Merlay III's grant on the north side of Morpeth

St Thomas' Well

Cottingburn

Staniflat

Roger de Merlay III's grant below the one on the north side of Morpeth, of 43 tofts

Newgate Street

Roger de Merlay III's grant of 16 tofts on Berhalvh

oldgate

market place

Roger de Merlay III's grant of 14 + 16 tofts related to Staniflat and Monksway

Bridge Street

chantry by 1294

mill by 1242

possible area of Roger de Merlay I's original grant before 1188

bridge by 1283

stone castle date uncertain

River Wansbeck

Fig 2.1

wooden castle

16

Fig 2.1

*Estimated locations of land grants by
Roger de Merlay lll as described in
charters of 1239 AD, upon which the new
borough of Morpeth was founded.*

Sources of place names
From 1239 charter
- *viam monacho*
- *Staniflat*
- *Berhalvh*

From 1852 map
- *Bailiff Butts*
- *Forster Bauk*

Monksway, Hodgson, 1832

In Roger de Merlay lll's second charter, he grants land to his free burgesses of Morpeth for the purpose of extending the borough. He granted all of the agricultural land, **on the north side of Morpeth**, from the Wansbeck on the west side of town, to the toft of Henry Doghet, and from that toft by the rivulet of the Cottingburn to the Well of St Thomas. Then it extends north from the well to Spen beyond Cottingburn, and as far as the dyke of the monks of Newminster to the west, and again to the Wansbeck.[12]

This is the area that I have suggested in my first created map, Fig 1.1, which may have been a meadow for the production of hay, and which I named the Newgate North block. It is narrow, running on both sides of the Cottingburn, so may not have had farmed strips running west/east across it. We can locate the rivers in the description, and St Thomas's well. The problems that remain are that we have no real idea where Henry Doghet's toft or Spen are.

The same charter then tells us that *below* that area, Roger de Merlay lll gave to the burgesses 43 tofts and half an acre of land, for the rent of 16 pence annually per toft, and for 2 pence the half rood.

I am estimating that this area of 43 tofts might be what I have called the Newgate South block. It is directly *below* the previous area, in the sense of southerly. These are long established west/east strips.

which is very beautifully written, contains a part of its seal, and is a gift from Roger de Merlay the Third to his free burgesses of Morpeth of all that culture of land on the north side of the town of Morpath, by the following boundaries—to wit—from the great river of Wanspic,* on the west side of the said town, to the toft of Henry Doghet, and from that toft by the rivulet of Cottingburne to the Well of St. Thomas, and from that well northwards to Spen by a certain march which the grantor had made for the said burgesses, and from Spen beyond Cottingburne as far as the dike of the monks of Newminster towards the west, and so by that dike to the great river of Wanspic; and below that culture, he gave to the said burgesses his 43 tofts and half an acre of land in free burgage to hold to them and their heirs of him and his heirs with all franchises and easements to the foresaid town appertaining, freely, quietly, and honourably, as was set forth in a charter which he had before granted to them, and by paying to him and his heirs 16d. annually for each full toft and for the half rood 2d. By the second of these deeds, which is probably the one alluded to in the first, the same Roger de Merlay the Third gave to the same free-burgesses, in free burgage, 46 tofts of his demesne lands in Morpath, that is—in the culture which was called Berhalvh, at the east end of the said town, 16 tofts; and in the culture called the Staniflat, between Cottingburne and the east side of the Monksway, 16 tofts; and between Cottingburn and the west side of the same way, 14 tofts, to hold to them and their heirs of him and his heirs with all liberties, customs, and easements to the said town of Morpeth belonging, by the annual payment of 16d. for each full toft.

2. Omnibʒ Rogerus de Merlay tertius . Nouerit uniūsitas ur̄a me dedisse libis burgensibʒ meis de Morpath totam culturam meam terre mee ex boreali pte uille de Morpath p has diuisas . scilicʒ. a magno flumine de Wanspic* in occidentali pte eiusdem uille usqᵿ ad toftum henrici doghet et ab eodem tofto p riuulum de Cottingburne usqᵿ ad fontem sc̄i Thome ᵗt ab eodem fonte uersus boream usqᵿ Spen p quandā diuisam qᵃm ego feci dc̄is burgensibʒ ᵗt de Spen ultᵃ Cottingburne usqᵿ ad fossetum monachoᴙ noui Monasterij versus occidentem et ita p illud fossetum usqᵿ ad magnū fluuium de Wanspic . Et infra dc̄am culturam dedi p̄dc̄is burgensibʒ meis qᵃdraginta tria tofta ᵗt dimid rodā in libero burgagio . Ha-

benda ᵗt tenenda sibi ᵗt heredibʒ suis de me ᵗt heredibʒ meis cum omn̄ibʒ libtatibʒ ᵗt aisiamtis p̄dc̄e ville de Morpath ptinentibʒ adeo libe ᵗt quiete ᵗt honorifice sicuti carta mea qᵃm dc̄i burgenses hn̄t de dono meo pportat ᵗt testatʳ. Reddendo inde annuati michi ᵗt heredibʒ meis ip̄i ut̄ heredes sui p quolibet plenario tofto sexdecim denarios ᵗt p dimid roda duos denarios . scitʒ. ad duos f̄minos . ad festū sc̄i cuthb̄ti in qᵃdragesimo dimid . ᵗt ad festū sc̄i Cuthb̄ti i Septemb̄ dimid . Et ego ᵗt heredes mei warantizabimᵍ ᵗtc. . Et ut hec donacio ᵗtc. . Hiis testibʒ dno Witto de Merlay . dno iohe de Plesseiz tū senescallo de Morpath . dno adā Bareth . dno Witto de Coiners . Ranulfo de Merlay . Witto fit Radulfi . Ricardo de Saltwic . et multis aliis.

3. Omnibʒ Rogerᵍ de Merlay f̄cius satm in dno . Sciatis me dedisse libis burgensibʒ meis de Morpath in libum burgagium quadraginta et sex toftos de dnico meo in Morpath . Scit in cultᵃra que vocatʳ Berhaluh ad capd orientale eiusdem uille ⫶ sexdecim toftos . Et in cultᵃra que vocatʳ Staniflat inf̄ Cottingburn ᵗt viam monachoᴙ ex pte orientali ⫶ sexdecim toftos . Et inf̄ Cottingburn ᵗt eandem viam ex pte occidentali ⫶ qᵃtuordecim toftos . Habēdos ᵗt tenendos illis ᵗt h̄edibʒ suis ⫶ de me ᵗt h̄edibʒ meis cū omn̄ibʒ libtatibʒ cōsuetudinibʒ ᵗt avsiamtis ad p̄dc̄am villam de Morpath ptinentibʒ . adeo libe ᵗt qiete in omn̄ibʒ sicuti carta mea qᵃm p̄di burgenses habent de dono meo ⫶ pleniᵍ pportat . Reddendo inde annuati michi ᵗt h̄edibʒ meis ip̄i ᵗt h̄edes sui p quolibet plenario tofto sexdecim denar̄ ad duos f̄minos . scit. mediatatem ad festum sc̄i Cuthberti in qᵃdragesimo ᵗt aliam medietatē ad festū sc̄i Cuthb̄i in Septembr̄ &c. &c. Hiis testibʒ dompno Ada tūc Abb̄e de nouo monastio Roḡo Bertᵃm de Bothal . Johe fit Sym̄ . Henr̄ Gateḡ . Johe de Plesset . Ada Barat . Thom̄ de Oggel . Ric̄ de Saltwic . Roḡo de Horset . Robto de Cam̄a . Bartholon̄ de Wyndegates . Witto de Cam̄a . Nichot de Scotton . Watto de Wytton et aliis.——*(Orig. in Town's Hutch.)*

4. Omnibus hōıbus hanc cartā visuris vel audituris Rogerus de Merlay tertius salutem . Noveritis me *audisse* cartam Rogeri de Merlay p̄ris mei in hec verba . Omnibus hōıbʒ has tras audituris &c. *(ut supra sub anno* 1180.) Quare volo concedo ᵗt confirmo pro me et heredibus meis p̄dictis burgensibus ᵗt heredibus suis quod habeant omnes libertates p̄dc̄as sicut carta Rogeri de Merlay p̄ris mei testatur ᵗt purportat . Et pretereo concessi pro me et heredibʒ meis quod nec prefati burgenses nec heredes eoᴙ tallientur nisi quando dn̄s rex talliabit burgos suos . et ad p̄mogenitū filiū meū milite faciendū

Fig 2.2 A selection from Hodgson's A History of Morpeth, describing Roger de Merlay's third charter in English, and the second and third charters in Latin. 13

In the third charter, Roger de Merlay lll gave another 46 tofts of his land to the burgesses, and the charter describes their situations. They are in three lots.

1. The farmed land called Berhalvh at the east end of the town. Here he gave 16 tofts. This looks like the area of short strips between the river and the Cottingburn, to the north of what became Bridge Street.

2. Land in Staniflat, between Cottingburn and the east side of Monksway. This land is related to the Stoney Flatts in later maps. Here he gave 16 tofts. There are problems here, because on later maps, Stoney Flatts is east of the Cottingburn. In the mid 1200s, the name might also have referred to land on the other side of the burn. The tofts were based on what became Bridge Street, as there are no burgages with buildings on the later Stoney Flatts.

3. Land between Cottingburn and the west side of Monksway. Here he gave 14 tofts. This one is a real puzzle. Where can land be that is *between* the Cottingburn, and the west side of Monksway? In view of all these difficulties, I am calling the 16 of the previous paragraph, and the 14 of this one, tofts related to Staniflat and Monksway, and placing them next to Berhalvh, on both sides of Bridge Street.

The spelling of Berhalvh is found in several variations. This is the one used in Hodgson's translation of the charter. He also spells it as Berehalgh on page 58 and on the charter it appears as Berhaluh. Berhalvh may mean *barley haugh*, a flat piece of land for growing barley, near a river.

Monksway is assumed by Hodgson to be Cottingwood Lane.[14] He probably translated this directly from the words *viam monacho* in the charter. The road runs south past St Thomas's Well. The well was located in what is now the Rotary garden next to the Methodist church.

I do realise that this map contains some wobbly estimates. I am sure that others have tried this before, and given up. I can understand why Hodgson, when he described the locations of the land grants, wrote: "These are the only notices and conjectures I will indulge in respecting the early years of Morpeth." It remains a challenge for future researchers.

Among the problems in deciphering the clues is the fact that place names and street names change over time. As these charters date from eight hundred years ago, before maps, when the people concerned knew the places intimately, descriptions would be clear to them which cannot be to us. There is also the possibility that mistakes have been transmitted in the documents, or that the Cottingburn has been significantly re-routed.

Some questions remain. Were the tofts already in existence, some even bearing houses, at the time Roger de Merlay "granted" them to the burgesses? Or were they measured out ready to give to prospective burgesses, based on the existing strips, but with no actual houses on them at that time?

The fact that Henry Doghet had a toft leans towards the first explanation. Perhaps there was a gradual movement towards establishing tofts across the strips, before the formal establishment of the charters.

On the other hand, all the land transactions in the borough annals recorded between tenants of the burgages take place *after* the charters of 1239.[15] This could be for a variety of reasons, but also could imply that no formal tenancies were established before Roger de Merlay lll's charters.

Perhaps it was a subtle change from the first situation to the second. We must allow that the answer requires further work.

It seems likely to me that the plans for these new tofts, the burgage plots, involved cutting wide new streets in both directions to the Market Place, streets which we now know as Bridge Street and Newgate Street, and the tofts were placed on both sides of the streets. The street of Oldgate may well already have existed. This is the time in which Roger de Merlay lll decided that it was worth sacrificing the agricultural strips, which brought him a minimal income, for the burgage plots from which he would get a much better return.

Whether or not this suggested map is close to the correct layout of the time, the town's burgage plots were finally established by Roger de Merlay lll. They were laid on some hundreds of strips which had been farmed until that time.

When the streets were cut through the strips, to peg out the tofts, the obvious natural divisions of the new plots already existed. There was an existing corrugated pattern of ridges. It must have been easier to use that pattern rather than to flatten it and measure a new one, and the significance of this practical arrangement has implications to the present day.

In the previous chapter, we learned that the long acre strips in Morpeth were composed of four strips each of about five yards wide. If we visualise this acre strip, thus divided lengthways, we come to the word *rood*. This word is used frequently in exchanges of tenancies in the following centuries, which we will look at in a later chapter.

Thus, if the burgess's toft was placed on a ridge five yards wide, and if its area of land extended the full furlong behind, it comprised a *rood*. If it extended a half furlong behind, it would comprise a half rood. Or if the toft was the width of two rigs, half a furlong behind, it would comprise one rood.

In Morpeth it seems that the five yard width of the ridge was retained, although the lengths were frequently cut through. The amazing thing is that, to this day, these widths can still be seen. This seemed to me to be the case from an examination of the map of 1852 and later maps. I used my acre model, divided into four rood widths, and moved it along Oldgate, Bridge Street and Newgate Street. Allowing for the hundreds of years of amalgamations and divisions, and for the fact that the ridges would not have been precision measured by the ploughmen, the five yard width was remarkably still visible at the time the maps were surveyed.

Wishing to see if what appeared on the maps still related to the present day situation, I measured a sample of street front properties in Newgate Street, between Appleby's bookshop and the alleyway beside T & G Allan, with a five yard rope, one Sunday morning.

Fig 2.3
Measuring the width of the shop
fronts in Newgate Street with a
five yard rope.

Ignoring the quizzical looks of passers-by, I found myself gasping in surprise at the close relationship between the five yard widths, and multiple or halves of five yards. I could almost picture Roger de Merlay III's retainers with their hammers and wooden pegs, laying out the boundaries, in 1239.

After the pegging out of the tofts, the ploughmen and their ox teams would be replaced by the new burgesses. The ancient echoes of their voices speaking their old English language are now but faint whispers in our path, as we make our way through the alleys of the town. We can share the pride they took as the neat rows of the furrows came together, and perhaps their resentment at the foreigners who took so much of the produce of their labour. They have gone, but they have left the traces of their work, if we care to find them.

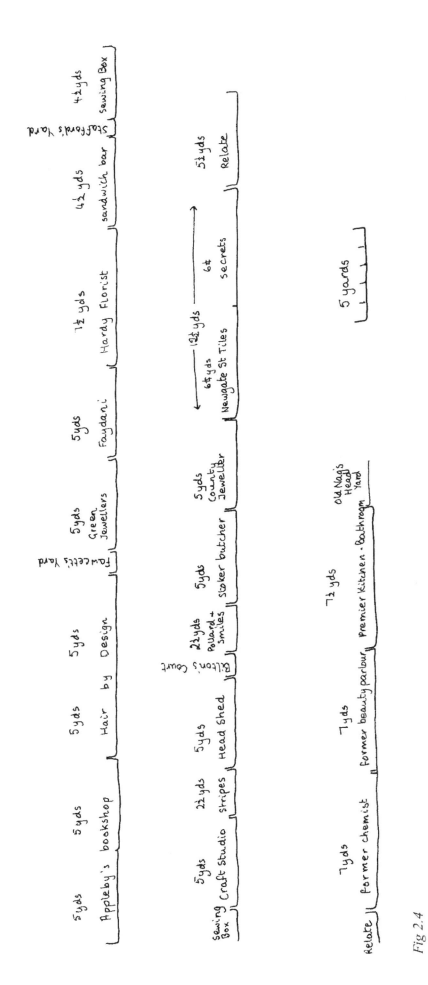

Fig 2.4

Shop fronts on Newgate Street, east side, from Appleby's Bookshop to Old Nag's Head Yard. The frequent five yard widths, and their multiples or halves, relate to the cut-through widths of the thirteenth century ploughed rigs

22

The barons of Morpeth were the wealthy people of their day. They were the descendants of the Normans who had obtained their land as a reward for their services in the conquest. They were going to enjoy their winnings. They could extract wealth from the lands they controlled, through the labouring of the conquered inhabitants.

They dominated the lands of their barony, and its population, and spoke their strange sounding French language. Some of the Morpeth barons married local women, who would have needed to learn French. William de Merlay, grandfather of Roger de Merlay l, married Menialda, a daughter of the local nobility, the Gospatrics. Ranulph de Merlay, their son, married Juliana, also a Gospatric, and her grandson Roger married Ada, daughter of the earl of Fife.[1] Thus the households of the de Merlays must have rung with both French and English. The women would have brought their own servants, and their own wet nurses. Their children must been rocked to sleep, and spoken to, in both languages.[2]

We cannot know how those Northumbrian women felt, who brought their inheritance as dowries to the Norman barons. Did they want to marry those foreign intruders? Was it a move up into a privileged lifestyle? Did Menialda speak to her little son Ranulph in English, and did he reply in French? Did Juliana in her turn learn French, so that she could speak to her children William, Roger and Osbert in their father's language? These women must have looked down over the fields being cultivated by the river, and wondered at their role.

Equally, the labourers in the fields below must have cast an occasional glance up at the castle, with fear, or envy. As Norman conquerors, the de Merlays were "castlemen who lived in large groups behind their walls and ditches, and subsisted on the tribute of sullen villagers."[3]

The barons however had responsibilities to the king. They were obliged to provide him with military assistance, for his battles in England, in Scotland and Wales, and in Normandy and France. This was an expensive business. Enjoying the good things of life, the newest fashions in weapons and armour, the pleasures of the chase and French wines required wealth too. Thus they were looking out for all possible sources of revenue.

The de Merlays, like all the other barons in Northumberland and the rest of England, belonged to a huge Norman controlled area, which extended from the Cheviots to the Pyrenees. They had family links in Normandy and other parts of France. They lived in a wider world than their immediate surroundings. They and their retainers moved around, and trade would have taken place.

Links between some of the Northumbrian baronies and their places of origin can be extracted from Percy Hedley's Northumberland Families, and I've located them on a map on Fig 3.1.

We do not know the place of origin of the de Merlays, or exactly how they became barons of Morpeth. However, we can extract the following from Percy Hedley's book, Northumbrian Families, and Hodgson's History of Morpeth.[4] Bishop William of Coutances was one of William the Conqueror's captains at the battle of Hastings in 1066. He was nominated the earl of Northumberland in 1080, but was able to confer this honour to his nephew Robert de Mowbray (spelled de Montbrai in Hedley's account). Hedley discusses that there may have been a family relationship between the de Mowbrays and the de Merlays. The barony of Morpeth may have been created by Robert de Mowbray while he was earl, and given to the de Merlays, in or around 1080.

Fig 3.1
Links between Morpeth, Northumberland, and the wider Norman-controlled lands in France.

The map shows it at its greatest after 1157, when Henry Duke of Anjou, future Henry ll of England, married Eleanor of Aquitaine.

The numbers show places of origin of some Northumbrian baronial families in Normandy and northern France.

1   Bailleul-en-Vimeu, Picardy
Barony of Bywell, the Baliol family (p 203)

2   Bolbec, near Le Havre
Barony of Styford, the Bolebec family (p24)

3   Bayeux. Odo Bishop of Bayeux was William the Conqueror's half brother. He ravaged Northumberland in 1080 (Kapelle p14)

4   Vassy, Calvados (p 198)
Barony of Alnwick, the de Vesci family

5   Coutances. The bishop of Coutances accompanied William the Conqueror and enabled the de Merlays to acquire the Morpeth barony

6   Laval, Mayenne (p 20)
Barony of Callerton, the Delaval family (p145)

Page numbers indicate source of this information in Percy Hedley's book Northumbrian Families.

By extracting a few clues from the Pedigree in Hodgson's History of Morpeth, Fig 3.1 above, we can gain further ideas of the links between the barons of Morpeth, and the wider demands of the French speaking kings of England, to whom they owed military duties. If the barons didn't want to support the king in his wars, they had to pay penalties. The de Merlays seemed to be less willing than the Greystocks, who later inherited the barony, to go off to France.[5]

Roger de Merlay l baron ? - 1188	in 1172 paid £4 scutage (a fine) for not going to Henry ll's war	Henry ll reigned 1154 - 1189
Roger de Merlay ll baron 1188-1239	in 1194 paid 20 marks to be excused for going to the wars in Normandy with Richard l	Richard l reigned 1189 – 1199
Roger de Merlay lll baron 1239-1266	in 1242 paid 50 marks not to join Henry lll's wars in Gascony (south west France)	Henry lll reigned 1216 - 1272
John de Greystock baron 1266-1306	maternal grandson of Roger de Merlay lll in 1294 went with Edward l to war in Gascony, and again a second time	Edward l reigned 1272 - 1307
William de Greystock baron 1342-1349	great grandson of John de Greystock 1342 went with Edward lll to war in Britanny 1342 – 1352 went frequently to wars in France and Gascony	Edward lll reigned 1327 – 1337 battle of Crécy 1346

Fig 3.2 The barons of Morpeth and their military connections with France.

What is most relevant to our story is their town building programme, which the de Merlays, like all the Northumbrian barons, began to undertake. This was happening throughout the area of France and England under the control of the Normans, and is fully described in Maurice Beresford's classic book, New Towns of the Middle Ages.

Establishing towns could be a good source of income. There was money to be made from rents, more than could be obtained from agriculture. Tolls could be charged at markets. Goods produced from the barons' own demesnes could be sold at profit. Tolls could be charged at bridges, mills and bakehouses. Fines from the court could go into their chests.

Like all new ventures, there were risks, and perhaps the younger generation would be impatient with the older. We can imagine a dialogue, in French of course, about the date of 1230, between the young Roger and his father Roger de Merlay ll.

The older man had established the market and the fair, at Morpeth, in 1199.

"But *mon pere*, we should enlarge the borough. Let's get rid of those pointless acres, where those annoying, slow villagers plod up and down in the mud, with their oxen. Let's plan lots of new opportunities for entrepreneurs to run businesses. We can measure up small tofts on the strips, invite people to build houses on them, and charge them hefty rents."

"*Mon fils*, I've created the market. I paid good money for it, and gave the king two good war horses. We have a slow but steady income from the land. Why change a good thing? No, I don't see the need to undertake any risky ventures."

But as soon as his father died, in 1239, the young Roger de Merlay lll took advantage of his freedom. To fully understand how the town was built upon the cultivated land next to the river, we can look at the larger picture. The town-building process going on in Morpeth was part of what was happening in the rest of Northumberland, as well as across England and France.

The new towns movement developed most strongly between the time of Henry I, who came to the throne in 1100 and that of Edward I, who died in 1307. Edward I himself established the new town of Berwick in 1296, after having first destroyed it while attacking the Scots.

The kings encouraged the barons to obtain royal charters for markets and to found new towns on their lands, as we've seen with the charters of the de Merlays in 1199 and 1239.

 As the barons held their properties through the theoretical licence of the sovereign, it was a good idea for them to obtain an agreement, a charter, from the king, which passed rights down to people at lower levels. It was not essential for the barons to obtain a charter, but it was a good idea. Maurice Beresford writes: "The greater fraction of wealth paid by the boroughs was a recognition not only of their wealthiness but of the indebtedness of the traders and craftsmen within them, to the Crown for providing good order and a good government."[6]

New towns in Northumberland

Suggested dates for **new towns** established
between 1147 – 1272

Newcastle upon Tyne	1080-1130
Mitford	1100 – 57
Alnmouth	1147, by this date
Morpeth	1199-1239
Felton	1200, around this date
Newbrough	1221
North Shields	1225
Warenmouth	1247
Newton in Warkworth	1249, by this date
Berwick	1296
Haydon Bridge	1323, around this date
Newbiggin*	1216-72
Alnwick*	1157-85

*There are some ambiguities as to whether or not these are new towns.

This list is taken from Maurice Beresford's New Towns of the Middle Ages, pages 469-475.

Fig 3.3

The barons tended to use a spare piece of land, often waste land, from which they had little benefit. They would then gain newer and higher rents. In Morpeth's case however, they placed their new town on fertile land under cultivation. This may have been because the land on the south side of the river, around the castle, is an awkward sloping area, not suitable for laying out a town.

Thus, the typical new town was formed. A section of land was portioned out, and subdivided into the new burgage plots, the tofts. A common pattern was to establish roads, or to create the plots on either side of an existing one. The plots were long and narrow, the short end on the street, with long strips of land behind, as in Morpeth.

A market was essential, this usually requiring a charter too. An early market at Morpeth may have existed in the time of Roger de Merlay l, but the first firm evidence we have is when Roger de Merlay ll obtained the market charter from King John in 1199. A borough was very unlikely to precede the market.[7]

The new towns were placed on the baron's land, but the bonded inhabitants themselves did not necessarily benefit from it. They were not normally the new burgesses. They remained in servitude to the baron, continuing to work the strips producing goods on his demesne or manorial land, and with time left over, working on their own strips for their personal survival.

At the market, the barons could sell their demesne produce, which was a stimulus for them to maximise its production. The new townspeople were potential customers. Outsiders would be charged a fee for selling their produce, although the burgesses were normally exempt.

Annual fairs were another opportunity for the baron to increase his income. They were an essential feature of new as well as existing towns.

As we have seen in my imaginary conversation earlier, the rents were relatively much higher for small tofts of expensive burgage land. Whereas a villager might pay four pence per acre, totalling ten shillings for his 30 acres, the burgess might owe one shilling for his small plot of perhaps one quarter of an acre, a rood. Rents from the burgesses were also much easier to collect.[8]

All the typical features of the new town, the mill, the bridge, the bakehouse, the prison and the court, which provided income for the baron, were present in Morpeth.

Who were the new burgesses, and where did they come from? Could the labouring ploughmen, in servitude to the barons, become freemen? Basically, that did not happen.

The new burgesses needed to be ambitious people, who had to be able to earn the rent for their plot. Not many of the ploughmen would have had the resources. The success of the town depended on skilled immigrants, men possessing knowledge of a craft or trade. They needed to be recruited quickly, sufficient in number to meet each other's needs, and to attract other sellers to the market. They might be skilled craftsmen from the countryside or nearby villages, who could sell their products in the market. Occasionally, refugee villagers, those who had fled from servitude in another barony, would take a plot. There was an accepted convention that unchallenged residence for a year and a day conferred freedom on a town-dweller.

The new burgess, once issued with his toft, was required to build his own house, and often within a time limit so that it was done quickly. Roger de Merlay lll would have estimated that he could attract new burgesses, although he could not be certain of being successful.

The sorts of skills required by the new burgesses were wide-ranging. They would include those of the clerk, carpenter, shoemaker, baker, butcher, tanner, smith, weaver, miller, washerwoman, brewer, forester, tailor and goldsmith. Craftsmen looking for an opportunity might be younger sons from other towns.[9]

There were many incentives to becoming a burgess. They had freedoms unknown to the villagers. They were able to sell or buy their tenancies, and move as their trades required them, even to other towns, an option unavailable to the unfree. Unlike the villagers, they had little or no obligation to labour for the baron. They were usually exempted from tolls in their borough, at the markets and fairs, and for the movement of their animals. In cases of dispute, they could attend the borough court rather than the manor court which would naturally operate for the benefit of the baron, and they organised their court themselves. They were free to form themselves into trade guilds to protect their rights. They could create more buildings on their plots, thus increasing their value.

We can see these features in Morpeth. Strong guilds became established. The burgesses were a tight-knit community, protecting themselves and their rights. They were able to develop their businesses and as they did so they established new buildings. The yards and alleyways behind the street frontages would start to appear.

Some of the towns which received charters failed to develop to any large extent. Not all the boroughs listed in Fig 3.3 became towns as successful as Morpeth. It probably helped that the town's location was on an important river crossing, on the main south/north route to Scotland.

The villagers gained little from the new town, and may have been worse off. Beresford puts it like this. He uses the word *seigneurs* for the nobility, and *villeins* for the bonded unfree inhabitants. "From 1150 to 1350, the main value of a village labour-force to the seigneurs was demonstrated when he had it working on his demesne. By showing how profitable it was to produce a surplus for the market, the very success of towns made seigneurs more aggressive in exacting the maximum effort from their rural labour-force. The villeins were conscripts on the lord's demesnes. Town air bred free, as the saying went; but the villeins who were bound to the soil, were able to breathe very little of it."[10]

We don't know exactly where the ploughmen of Morpeth and their families lived, when they were excluded from the process. The de Merlays and their descendants would still have required them to work on the demesne. Perhaps they lived in crude hovels on the south side of the river, around the castle and the church, where the lords of the manor still retained large open fields. Perhaps they looked across the Wansbeck with envy at the lucky burgesses within, while the barons tightened up their working conditions in order to have as much produce as possible for the new market in Morpeth. Meanwhile, from their stronghold on the hill, the de Merlays enjoyed the good things of life, the wines, the hunting expeditions and the feasting, and the burgesses got on with developing trade in the town.

Taking the bread to the bakehouse, 1664

4   Burgesses amid the conflicts 1260 – 1604 – 1830
Making boots and baking bread as the armies pass through

The new burgesses of Morpeth earned their living through the trades of a market town, over the following centuries. They were butchers and skinners, tanners and curriers, fullers and weavers. They reared, bought and sold animals, killed them, and crafted produce for sale. Wheat and other arable crops were grown, harvested, milled and baked into bread.

There was never much peace in this border county between Scotland and England. The armies which passed through would kill and burn, sometimes gaining and other times losing. They often used the main route to the north and the river crossing in Morpeth. This had been the case in the first two hundred years after the Norman conquest, and continued throughout the middle ages.

From the town annals, faithfully reproduced by John Hodgson in his History of Morpeth, we can follow the recorded events that took place after the 1239 charter of Roger de Merlay lll up to 1832, when he compiled his book. Any of the following points in this chapter, not otherwise referenced, can be found in the annals under the appropriate date, between pages 115 and 170.

Despite a litany of skirmishes and battles, the annals record the affairs of the borough with a seeming calmness. Hodgson records land transactions and court appearances, and occasional glimpses of daily life. From them, we can get some insight into the lives of the people who slowly but surely built up the town. We can also look at a study of the guilds into which the burgesses organised themselves. And a map in 1604 gives us some glimpses of how the town had developed from the first charters.

After the earliest charters, there are some entries in the annals which illustrate the balance of power between the burgesses and the lord of the manor. In Roger de Merlay lll's first charter of 1239, he had allowed the burgesses to pasture their animals on his wheat stubbles in the north part of the town, except for the first fifteen days after the corn was taken away. This may have been so that his labourers could glean the valuable remaining grain for himself. He also outlined how much the burgesses had to pay for taking turf from his turbaries, and for grazing their animals in his fields. When he granted them the market, he reserved for himself the toft of Alice Hudde, a workshop, and the town's bakehouse. The burgesses and their wives had to grind their corn at his mill in Morpeth, paying him a *multure* of one sack of flour for every 13 milled.[1]

In 1282, the burgesses signed a new agreement with him, which obliged them to grind their corn only at the lord's mill, paying one twentieth of the flour thus produced as payment. It looks like they had managed to successfully negotiate the rate downwards.

Countless entries in the annals between 1244 and the late 1500s refer to land transactions of the burgage plots. Because they did not use maps, the transfers describe the plot by others on the boundaries. For example, in 1296, "William, son of Ralph Bateman of Morpeth, gave Isabella Bateman, his sister, a burgage in Morpeth, lying between the land of Henry of the Bakehouse on the one side, and that of Christian of the Boyt on the other."

In 1296, King Edward l passed through Northumberland, probably through Morpeth, on his way to hammer the Scots. He brutally captured and sacked Berwick. A Scottish army was crushed at Dunbar, and the Stone of Destiny was removed from Scone to Westminster.[2] We can be sure that the Stone would have passed through Morpeth, and wonder if this event was remarked upon by the inhabitants of that time.

Edward's armies must have trampled along the new streets of Morpeth, between the tofts, observed by the burgesses. We see that in 1301, the king was at Morpeth on June 28, on his way to Scotland again, and on the 19th of February the following year, he was at Felton on the way back. In 1305, he was back again, settling tofts and land in his ownership in Morpeth on the chaplains of the Chantry, so that they would say masses for the souls of himself, his ancestors and all the faithful departed.

During his reign between 1307 and 1329, Robert Bruce, King Robert l of Scotland, "inflicted upon Northumberland the darkest and most miserable conditions it has ever had to endure."[3] Despite the atrocities and tediously complex struggles recorded by Richard Lomas in his book County of Conflict, the annals of Morpeth record a series of peaceable land transactions, in which roods of land are passed from one tenant to another. Many gifts and donations are made to the Chantry chapel; for example, in 1335, "two roods and two parts of one rood of a burgage in Morpeth ... to hold of him and his successors chaplains celebrating divine services in the said chapel of All Saints, in Morpath, for the soul of Master Richard of Morpath", by paying eight shillings, and increasing every year by two shillings up to 16 shillings.

During the reign of Edward lll, from 1327 to 1337, the endless campaigns between England and Scotland ranged again over Northumberland, including the crushing of the Scots at the Battle of Halidon Hill, just north of Berwick in 1330. In 1337, the Scottish King David raided Northumberland as far as the South Tyne, and Hexham was devastated in 1346.[4] Morpeth families must have heard about this, and shivered at nights in their feather beds, or the poorer ones on their heaps of straw.

As well as the wars between England and Scotland, the wars in France were continuing. As we've seen, the barons of Morpeth accompanied Edward l and Edward lll to their wars in France. William de Greystock was frequently in France between 1342 and 1352, and the battle of Crécy was in 1346.

Whether or not any of the local people, the burgesses or the more humble workmen, found themselves drawn into these battles, the annals of Morpeth do not record. The Battle of Otterburn took place in 1388, but despite this event, nothing more significant occurs between 1384 and 1389 than the transferring of a waste rood of land, and a dispute between the men of Morpeth and Mitford over a moor.

After 1400, there is a change in the way the burgage plots are described in the annals, and this may relate to how the tofts on the old strips were evolving. The new word used is *tenement* rather than *burgage* in the land transactions. We find it used about a property in Newgate Steet in 1391, twice in 1400, twice again in 1403, and frequently after that. We can't be certain what the writers meant by this term, but it is likely that it was a property with a set of buildings on it, rather than a single house at the end of the strip. It could indicate the infilling of the land behind the main street, the beginnings of what later became called the *yards*. Property transfers were still often measured in roods or parts of roods, the old field strips being still the basis of the boundaries.

In 1402, Henry lV left Newcastle in August, on his campaign to Scotland, and was back in that city a month later. The most likely route was through Morpeth. Harry Hotspur revenged his defeat at Otterburn by capturing the Earl of Douglas on the slopes of Hamildon Hill near Wooler.

And so it goes on, the endless marching back and forth across the county, the ransackings, the revenge attacks, all of which must have caused sufferings to families everywhere.[5]

By about 1466, the word *tenement* becomes the usual term for referring to land transactions. The people in the town were conducting established businesses by then. Despite the passing of armies, daily life in the borough of Morpeth was going on.

The guilds

The burgesses were organising themselves into guilds, according to their trades. Guilds were rather like early trades unions. They protected their members and their rights. They controlled those who could join their trade, and prices of the goods. They were very jealous of their privileges, and although they trained apprentices, they and unskilled labourers of a lower status would have been given inferior accommodation, behind the main house, over a stable, or in lofts or cellars. In 1530, we learn of a land exchange in the marketplace to Umfra Dave, a glover, of "two shops, and a loft upon them, in the M'kgatsted".

The most detailed account of the guilds in Morpeth can be found in the booklet, The Medieval Guilds of Morpeth, by Roland Bibby. He points out that although the earliest surviving bye-laws of the cordwainers' guild date from 1470, guilds must have existed a considerable time before then.[6]

The guild members were burgesses, and they held their burgage plots in legal tenure. Among their privileges was that of belonging to the Corporation, which was the ruling council of the borough. These were the people of influence.

The guild members controlled their apprentices with an iron glove. The young men were not allowed to leave a master without reasonable cause. We can picture the youthful apprentices, in their living quarters behind the main houses, becoming "haughty minded, high stomached and wanton conditioned … less obedient and serviable … not knowing their duty to their superiors."[7]

The bye-laws of the early guild members included not being able to employ a Scotsman in any way, the compulsory attending of the monthly meetings and the annual procession to the church of St Mary. Later rules forbade "going to make shoues in the countrey", selling from stalls on market day, instead of from their shops; and failing to provide "sufficient dinner" for the members on their agreeing to set up shop.[8]

The links between them and the land around the town remained strong. As the burgesses developed their trades, their lives were still involved with the land. They needed animals, oxen and horses, which they would have grazed on the commons, and some of them would have grown wheat or barley in the fields around the town. For these activities they would pay dues to the lord of the manor. In 1266, at the death of Roger de Merlay lll, an inquest found that the burgesses of Morpeth had paid him a total of £10 per year in rent for their borough, as well as sums for use of a salmon fishery, and grazing on Cottingwood and the East Park.

It is not easy to discern from the annals any influence the abbey and the monks of Newminster had. In 1343 there were ten or more land transfers to them, in 1364 twenty three, and in 1389 fourteen. The income from the tenancies would have gone to the abbey.[9] The dissolution of the abbey of Newminster in the 1530s doesn't appear in the annals. There doesn't seem to be any sense that the end of the abbey caused much distress to the town, which seems rather surprising. In fact, there is an account that the king's commissioners triumphed, and the abbey was razed to the ground "with the aid of a mob from Morpeth."[10] If this is true, the mob could only be composed of the burgesses and/or their apprentices and other employees. It gives a rather different idea from the rather pompous and proper guildsmen, who enjoyed a good dinner, liked processions, and ruled their apprentices with rigour.

The 1400s and 1500s were the times of cross-border local and national conflicts like the Battle of Flodden which took place in 1513. The lord of the manor of Morpeth, Lord Thomas Dacre, was the warden of the West March. He was responsible to the English Crown for controlling the western border between England and Scotland.

He was not resident at Morpeth, but he used his gaol here, from which the prisoners escaped only too often.[11]

There is a story from Flodden that he "found the body of the King of Scots under a heap of his slaughtered warriors".[12] Whether true or not, he later entertained the Scottish king's widow in Morpeth. King James lV of Scotland had married Margaret, the sister of Henry Vlll.

In the year after the battle of Flodden, she married Archibald Douglas, the 6th Earl of Angus. Soon after that, she fled Scotland. At this time, "the quene was seik in Morpeth in Ingland, perrell of her lyffe." Hodgson comments that she probably resided in Morpeth castle till Lord Dacre found her an asylum in Harbottle castle, where she gave birth to Douglas's child.[13]

It must have been a matter of gossip and interest to all the townspeople, having royalty in their town. Queen Margaret spent most of 1515 to 1516 in Morpeth castle. She had 22 gowns of gold and silk cloth in her apartments, and had sent to Edinburgh for more.[14]

A little later, in 1523, Lord Dacre found time to re-organise the guilds of Morpeth. From twenty four small guilds, seven major crafts were selected. The smaller crafts were clustered around the larger to make groups of a similar size.

The seven guilds included a range of trades, each with their coat of arms.

- Merchants, included tailors, barbers, wigmakers, bowyers (bowmakers), fletchers (arrowmakers)

- Tanners were paired with barkers, who supplied oak bark for the tanning process

- Fullers, with dyers, wrights, carvers and hatters

- Smiths, with saddlers, slaters, loriners (saddlery metalworkers), sword slippers (scabbard-makers)

- Cordwainers (shoemakers) with curriers (dressers of tanned leather)

- Weavers and skinners, with glovers and butchers.

Each guild produced a certain number of its members for admission to the Corporation, to a total of twenty four. New burgesses could be appointed. Together with the bailiffs, who were elected by the Corporation, they were the effective town council.[15]

Further interest for the borough residents occurred in 1547, when a daring rescue took place in their town. The Earl of Huntley, the Lord Chancellor of Scotland, was imprisoned in

Morpeth. On Christmas Eve, a "gentill man called George Kar, bordurar, come to ye town of Morpeth the nyght, with two guid horses, and awaitit at the back syd of the toune."

The Earl knew that his rescue was coming, and waited for the signal, while playing cards with Sir Rauf Avane, "his kepar". He mystified Sir Rauf with these words:

> "Ane mirk nycht,
> "Ane wearie knycht
> "Ane wilsum way
> "And knowis not quahair to go
> "God be my gyd."

He told the puzzled Sir Rauf that this was an ancient saying in Scotland, and "entered into the cartes again." Then "he gaif his place to ane uther to play for him, and past as it were to do sum necesser effaris of his awin," and escaped with his servant Johne Innes at the "back duire of the ludgeing". He managed to cross the "bordouris of Inglande" and get to Edinburgh where he joined his wife.

Such a daring escape, as well as the little rhyme, must have been gossiped about in the town.

These were the unsettled years of the border reivers. They were the families from both sides of the border, who continually harried each other, stealing their cattle and burning their houses. Morpeth was lucky in this respect, not being the main focus of the raids. They took place more to the north and west, in the Tynedale and Redesdale areas. There were nevertheless various forays. In 1558, 1570 and 1590 Scottish raiders penetrated as far south as Morpeth. Alec Tweddle remarks that "the mazes, alleys, barns, buildings and stockyards situated along the lines of the burgage strips would no doubt also contribute to the defences of what was in essence still a medieval town".[16] This could be the case, but equally, a town with many barns filled with straw and hay, houses thatched with heather roofs, and no strong surrounding walls must have been an easy target.

The title of lord of the manor of Morpeth passed through a series of family changes. Roger de Merlay lll and his wife had had no sons, and the manor of Morpeth thus passed to the Greystocks in 1271, through the marriage of their daughter Mary to William, baron of Greystock in Cumbria.

In the fifteenth century, once again through the lack of a male heir, Morpeth passed to the Dacres on the marriage of Elizabeth Greystock to Baron Thomas Dacre.

In 1577, Lord William Howard of Naworth in present day Cumbria married heiress Elizabeth Dacre, and claimed the share of her estates which included Morpeth. Tumultuous proceedings followed, with the involvement of Queen Elizabeth l. Eventually, after Dacre being accused and then acquitted of treason, and Howard spending time in the Tower of London, Morpeth passed to the Howards in 1601, where it remained for nearly three centuries.

The bailiffs and burgesses were obliged to acknowledge Lord William Howard's rights as lord of the manor, although they had sided originally with the Dacres. In what is perhaps a token of goodwill towards them, "Belted Will" presented the borough with a silver mace in 1604. It is in the mayor's parlour to this day, and used on civic occasions.[17]

1604 – the first map of Morpeth

The year of 1604 is an important year for Morpeth in another respect, as Lord William Howard commissioned a map to be made of his newly acquired lands and the borough of the town. He needed to know exactly what he owned, and commissioned the surveyor whose Latin name is Gulielmus Haiwarde, and whose English name is William Haiwarde, for the job. This is the first useful historic map of Morpeth. Two versions of it exist, dated 1603 and 1604. Hodgson describes a 1603 map as smoky, dusty and faded. The one reproduced here is a 1604 version, in Fig 4.1. From it, we can see what the town of Morpeth looked like.

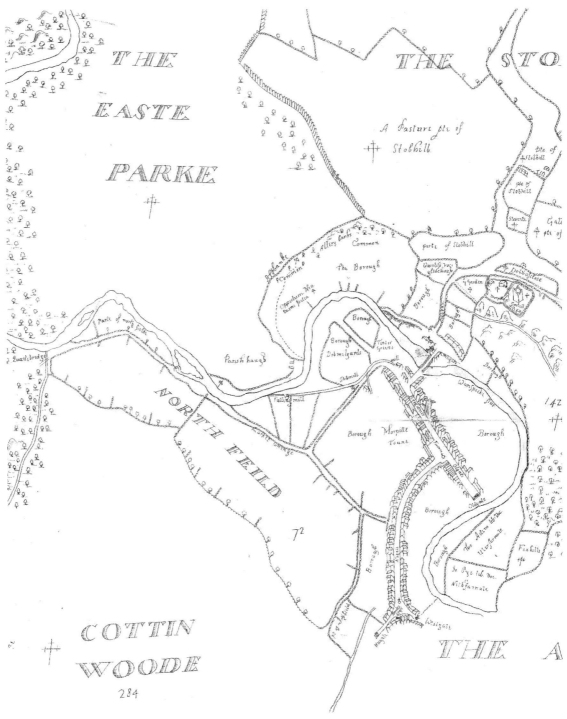

Fig 4.1
The 1604 map by William Haiwarde for Lord William Howard.
Courtesy of the Society of Antiquaries of Newcastle upon Tyne.

The first and most obvious thing we notice, besides the curious south-easterly orientation, is the street layout. Brigstreete, Olgate and Nugate are named. These are our Bridge Street, Oldgate and Newgate Street. There appears to be gates or barriers at the ends of Oldgate, Newgate and Westgate, and a possible tower at the south end of the stone bridge.

The drawing of the little houses is likely to be indicative rather than an exact number. It is improbable that that there were only seven properties on the north side of Oldgate, or about thirteen along the north side of Bridge Street. The map-maker is thus creating an impression of the town. It does show a lesser concentration of properties along the south side of Oldgate, which may mean that this area was more intensively cultivated.

There are only a few indications of the development of buildings and yards behind the main street. There is a suggestion of two buildings behind the main street fronts on the east side of Newgate Street and one on the west side. Similarly one or two others may be deduced behind Bridge Street and Oldgate.

The houses are placed side by side, without spaces between, which indicates continuous street fronts, rather than separate houses with gardens.

The fields behind the three main streets are left blank, and are marked *borough*. The map-maker has made no attempt to show the burgage plots, but equally we can see that there were no specific buildings or street development to the rear. Other than the suggestion of buildings behind those on the main streets, we cannot learn from this map how much development there was, in 1604, of the yards and alleyways.

A count of the total number of properties comes to about 130, which includes 12 on the south side of the river. Some of the roofs were probably not houses, but the number of 130 could be meant to indicate how many burgesses there were in the town, or it could be a co-incidence.

We can also see a tower-like structure within the castle walls, in its current location. There is a big building, probably Lord Dacre's gaol, on the south side of Bridge Street, and roughly where the present day Old Gaol Yard is.

The curious cross shape with ticks on three of its sides found in the surrounding fields indicates *demesne* lands, those in the ownership of the new lord of the manor. Nine open fields, not marked with this cross, are named as belonging to the borough.

North Feild, as the map spells it, is not named as either *borough* or *demesne*. Perhaps it was rented out to various burgesses. There is no indication of how any of the land was farmed. The attached Fig 4.1 is only a selection of the map. In the complete version, we can see the great fields of The Easte Parke, The West Parke, The Stobhill, Cottin Woode and The Abbie Groundes. By this time, the abbey had been dissolved, but the name apparently continued. We have conjectured earlier that the east and west parks may have been the other two great fields of the farming system of which North Field was one, which by this time might have become converted to pasture.

Besides the obvious three main streets, there are some other routes through the central area of the town. The road from the east is named as Market Loninge, meaning Market Lane. It runs as far west as Newgate Street, and has its obvious destination as the Market Place. A narrower roadway turns northward towards Cottin Woode, along what was referred to in the de Merlay charters as Monksway, now Cottingwood Lane. The little hedge or track which turns westward from this roadway, crossing the Cottingburne, could have been an ancient route to Newminster, and is still the little thoroughfare we now call Beggars' Lane. There is a route from Market Loninge to the dobmill, where bleaching took place, and routes or hedges towards the fulling mill, where wool was treated.

The church and the rectory are well away from the main centre of the town, with only a few properties close by. (See Appendix 1.) The earliest foundation of Morpeth, centred around the original 1080 castle and the church, has been well surpassed by the new borough established by the de Merlays on the fields to the north, in the 1200s.

We may deduce then that within the basic layout of the three main streets of Oldgate, Bridge Street and Newgate Street, town life went on, buildings being utilised behind the frontages, until we see illustrated the full development of the back areas in the maps of the nineteenth century.

After 1604, a few items from the annals may give us a flavour of everyday life in the town. From this time onwards, the annals have changed significantly. They still contain details of land transactions, and they list the bailiffs as they changed, but there are a few colourful incidents described from the court leets, and items of news.

The burgesses were still struggling to assert their rights against those of the lord of the manor. In 1618, they had to eat humble pie, after challenging Lord William Howard on several issues. They had to agree that they "hold the pasture of ground called Cottingwood" only at his will, and "whatever we have heretofore done to the contrary" done it "merely out of ignorance… for which in all humility we do acknowledge". Similarly, the burgesses found themselves obliged to send any of the inhabitants of Morpeth to the lord's court if they were found to grind their corn anywhere but the lord's mills. They had to acknowledge that the courts, fairs and markets belonged to Lord William, and that they had no title to them. It was all very humiliating. "And we hereby further covenant unto the said lord Wm and his heirs never hereafter to attempt to possess the premises." After much similar mortifying language, their pride was saved a little in the last paragraph where "we claim to be a corporation … in such manner and form as our predecessors formerly claimed the same." This was signed by bailiffs, the serjeant, seven aldermen and eleven freemen.

The annals record a battle which took place in Morpeth. During the Civil War, in May 1644, Scottish Parliamentary troops under General Leslie took the castle. It was then besieged and retaken by Scottish Royalist troops under the Earl of Montrose. Montrose was later defeated in 1645 by General Leslie, at the battle of Philiphaugh near Peebles, where his troops were slaughtered, including three hundred Irish women and children who had followed their men to the battle.[18] If the people of Morpeth learned about this, they must have discussed it over their good dinners.

In 1661, the current lord of the manor, Charles Howard, was appointed the first Earl of Carlisle. Thus the inhabitants had to accustom themselves to a new name again for their overlord.

The restoration of King Charles ll to the throne affected Morpeth, in that the king issued a new charter to the Corporation of the town in 1662, for which they paid a fine of ten pounds. This was perhaps more to ensure loyalty to himself, rather than to do the town any favours. Hodgson calls it "one of the antient royal methods of raising the wind".

Some unfortunate inhabitants were presented at the court leet on the first of September 1664, for not grinding at the lord's mill, for not baking at the lord's common bakehouse, for keeping swine contrary to order, for keeping common middings (presumably middens) before their doors, and for not keeping their fronts clean. These court appearances are touching and homely. If you ground your wheat in your hand mill at home, or you baked your bread secretively in your own hearth, you were fined. And if you wanted a bit of bacon to feed the family over the winter, you had better get permission.

The annals record that the plague visited the town in 1665, and people fled to Cottingwood. The bodies of those who died were buried on the Quarry Bank, near the steep road out of Morpeth to the east.

The houses of the town were frequently subject to fires. We read of fires in 1676, 1686 and the worst of all in 1689, when fifty dwelling houses, with kilns, barns, stables and outhouses were burnt down in the space of three hours.

A quick backward look at a 1515 entry in the annals describes housebuilding materials, which helps us understand the fire risk. In that year, Robert Trewick of Morpeth, weaver, and Joan his wife, leased a tenement in Aldgate Street, and were charged within the next two and a half years to "beld and mak-of-new a house of foure cupelles with balkes, sparres and other tymber work …and the walles of the highte of seven ffoote of stone and mortar sufficiauntly , with wyndoe and dores, and to theke the same house with hedder and straw …" We can only guess what what *cupelles* are, but the *theke* must be thatch, of heather and straw.

The Jacobite rebellions in 1715 and 1745 didn't leave Morpeth untouched. Once again, the town's location on the main north/south route meant that armies were marching through.

The Hanoverian protestant King George 1 was on the throne. Some of the Northumbrian gentry supported the cause of the King Over the Water, James lll, who was living in France. The noblemen were planning his restoration, and preparing for an invasion in Northumberland. A prominent Jacobite Northumbrian, General Thomas Forster, led his army of 335 men through Morpeth in October 1715, with the intention of taking Newcastle. He proclaimed King James lll as king in Morpeth marketplace. His army was described at the time by his opponent General Carpenter. "Many of them are mean men and have worse horses and are much dispirited."[19]

Morpeth's inhabitants did not necessarily support this declaration. The town had sent two Whig members to parliament in 1713, and the Whigs supported King George.

However many townspeople would have heard the proclamation, trumpeted by a William Ossington, and doubtless whispered together over their ale.

The annals don't mention the declaration. There is though a brief mention in 1745 that General Wade's army, camped on Cottingwood, was supplied from the town with hay and straw and other requisites, in the time of the second Jacobite rebellion.

In 1746, after the crushing of the Stuart cause, we find that the protestant Prince of Hesse was received by an assembly of magistrates, gentry and clergy in Morpeth. This was to the general satisfaction, so the annals record, of all ranks of the people, and concluded with "many public worthy healths at the Cross, bonefires, repeated peals of bells, loud huzzas, and all possible variety of loyalty."

During the 1730s and 1740s, the annals report a few incidents showing the prevailing moral standards of the townspeople. Poor Mary Coxon was denounced in church in for the crime of fornication, and excommunicated. It wasn't only the women were thus penalised, as we find William Storey having to stand in a high place, in "his penetential habit", with "a white sheet on, and a rod in his hand", again for the grievous sin of fornication.

In 1741, Elizabeth Holburn had to stand at the market cross for two hours, wearing the *branks*. This unpleasant object can still be seen in the historic council chamber in Morpeth Town Hall. It is a metal frame which goes over the head, with a metal blade which was inserted into the mouth to prevent the wearing from speaking. It was a punishment for bad language, perhaps for scolding. Elizabeth had committed the heinous crime of using "scandalous and opprobrious language to several persons in the town, as well as to the bailiffs". I wonder what her husband Thomas thought of this punishment.

Then, in 1743, a wicked "scotchwoman" stole two tablecloths and eight napkins, and a hen "drest for the spit" from the butcher. The bailiffs "immediately sent her to the clock-house and whipt her the next day". The clock-house here must be the Clock Tower, constructed by this time (it does not appear on the 1604 map), which acted for some time as a town lock-up.

Some prisoners escaped from the big gaol in 1789, having sawn off their irons, forced the inner door, knocked down the turnkey, and imprisoned the gaoler in their own ward. The artillery was called however, and they were "brought to submission and made secure".

A little domestic touch is shown in 1800, when Barbara and Margaret Purdy were washing their vegetables in the Wansbeck, near Bowles Green (Buller's Green). The lack of plentiful running water beside the houses would mean it was easier to take the garden produce to the water, rather than carrying water. Unfortunately, one of the women fell in the water, and the other attempted to save her. But both were hurried down the stream, and drowned.

Referring to the 1604 map, in 1832 Hodgson was able to say: "The town itself was very little less then than it is now. Indeed the only additions it seems to have received in modern times are, a few houses on the east side of Newgate, called *Union-street*; and some north of Bridge Street, called King-street. Its principal source of wealth is from its large cattle markets; but even with these, which are only of about a century's duration, it is not in a flourishing state."

These few snippets from the annals, and an examination of the 1604 map, have revealed the life of a country town not changing greatly as the centuries passed by. Once the burgage plots had been laid out on the old agricultural strips, its pattern and lifestyle was largely unchanging. People worked at their trades, sold their goods, raised their families, were witnesses to the passing of the armies and the name changes of the absent lords of the manor, and got on with their lives as they had always done.

5   Slums on the riggs   1830 – 1930
Life and death in the yards and alleyways

"If any person shall permit to flow any night-soil, offal, putrid meat or fish, entrails of fish, carrion, dead animals, blood, dung, manure, oyster shells, bones, broken glass, china or earthenware, dust, ashes, refuse of vegetables or fruits, dirty water or any other offensive matter upon any street, court, highway, alley, footpath, he shall for each offence pay a fine not exceeding two pounds."[1]

This extraction is from the bye-laws of 1841. Queen Victoria had come to the throne in 1837. The ploughmen and their families have long disappeared. The craft burgesses and their employees are merging into shopkeepers and publicans, owners and workmen in tan yards, mills and manufactories. Horse drawn transport is prominent. The cattle market has become of great importance. The population is increasing, and the market town is becoming an unpleasant place in which to live. A dense network of buildings is growing up in the yards and alleyways behind the main streets, and on the Back Riggs.

The bye-laws tell us more. After nine in the morning, the inhabitants were forbidden to shake carpets or mats there, to roll or drag wagons or carcasses of animals along the public passageways, and to ride or drive horses or cattle through them, except for cattle on market day.

There was a fine of maximum £3 if they impeded movement by any of the following activities. They must not:

- hang out goods for sale
- hang out washing
- fly a kite, slide or skate
- make a bonfire
- set off fireworks
- play football or bowls.

Obviously the children had been having too riotous a time.

Heavy though the fine seems to be for such minor offences, it is less stringent on those who "wilfully and indecently expose his or her person", where the fine was a maximum of only £2.

If you lived on the ground floor of what were now tenements, you had the unpleasant responsibility of cleaning the channels, drains, gutters and sewers adjacent to your property, if they passed across, over or under where you lived. Failure to do so resulted in a maximum fine of £5.

All these rules display a picture of unsanitary and crowded living areas. The yards contained long rows of buildings, houses, wash-houses, workshops, sheds, privies, stables and coach-houses, all crowded alongside each other, with little light penetrating, and with open drains or sink stones throughout.

The poor women of the town did their best. A government inspector did give credit where he could. "The cottages throughout the town are clean where the inhabitants have any facilities for preserving them so. The floors in general are of stone, and after having been washed, it is the practice to sprinkle them over with white sand."[2]

Yards bustling with people and animals, 19th century

We can pity the hard-working women whose job it was to keep the houses tidy. In 1851, there were 516 women in Morpeth working outside the home, the vast majority in low-prestige occupations. Two hundred and ninety three women were working in domestic service, or as washerwomen. One hundred and thirty were involved with the making and selling of food and drink. Fifty one were sewing clothes or shoe-making. There were 11 teachers, and 31 were employed in agriculture.[3]

Imagine trying to feed and clean the children after a day at tasks like those, not to mention dealing with your own pregnancy and childbirth, caring for the helpless elderly relations, and then trying to wash the floors and sprinkle them with sand!

The men in the same year ranged across a variety of occupations, the largest number in 1851 being agricultural labourers,107, followed by shoemakers, 90, and then gardeners and seedsmen, 56. By 1891, there were 117 men employed as coal miners, and 104 as gardeners and seedsmen.[4]

Population statistics for Morpeth township, available on the Northumberland Communities website, show us the following:

1801 – 2951
1821 – 3415
1861 – 4521
1881 – 5068.

By the mid nineteenth century, the word *yard* was appearing in addresses. In other towns, we find narrow alleys and yard areas named as *court* or *close or chare*. In Morpeth, we find those too, with Percy Court, Sweetbriar Close and Copper Chare. *Yard* however is the most common.

Who were the people who lived in the yards? "Rich and poor lived cheek by jowl in the mid-nineteenth century ... Not one exclusively middle-class street can be identified before the 1850s, when Howard Street, 'a fine row of buildings, and Dacre Street, which consisted of dwellings of a 'superior character' were built."[5]

The burgesses thus must have still lived in the big houses on the main streets until the 1850s. The less well off lived, as always, in lofts or cellars, or behind, in the yards. On a list of nearly 300 burgesses of the borough of 4th September 1848, twenty four lived in the yards. Of them, many lived in yards behind public houses, including the Turk's Head, the Scotch Arms, the Old King's Head, the George and Dragon, the Earl Grey and the Wheatsheaf. Others lived in yards which were named after the owners of the buildings likely to be on the main street, Stoker's Yard, Bell's Yard, Bowser's Court, Chatto's Yard and Forrest's Buildings. There was also one from Percy Court, four from Corporation Yard, and five from Back Riggs.[6]

As for the population, they earned their living in all the variety of ways one would expect, in a market town in a rural area. In the 1822 (or 1828, there is some debate about the date) Pigot's Directory of Northumberland, listed trades include blacksmiths; boot, shoe, clog and patten makers; grocers and tea dealers; milliners and dressmakers; cabinet makers, cartwrights and joiners; butchers, skinners and tanners; tailors, linen weavers and drapers; and many more. Most of their addresses are on the main streets, Bridge Street, Newgate Street and Oldgate.

However, as this story is focussing on the yards, here is a list from the directory of the trades being carried out in them.

- auctioneers - Turk's Head Yard and Percy Court
- baker - Thompson's Buildings
- blacksmiths - Wheatsheaf Yard, Scotch Arms Yard, Turk's Head Yard
- brewer – Back Riggs
- butcher – Bell's Yard
- gardeners and seedsmen – Back Riggs
- glover – Bell's Yard
- joiners – Bowser's Yard, Scotch Arms Yard
- milliner and dressmaker – Bell's Yard
- painter and glazier – Hodgson's Yard
- rope and twine maker – Thompson's Buildings
- tailors – Hodgson's Yard, George and Dragon Yard.

Morpeth people, and country people coming in for the market, could thus purchase many of their needs in the network of alleyways, perhaps where prices were lower reflecting back street rents.

We can get detailed pictures of the crowded nature of the town in the nineteenth century from the maps of the time. There are four, all drawn to the highest standard, and to a similar scale, at or around 25 inches to the mile, or 1:2500. They are:

1826 J Wood's Plan of the Town of Morpeth   (Appendix 2)
1852 Plan of the Town of Morpeth, for the Local Board of Health   (App 3, Fig 1.3)
1860 First Edition Ordnance Survey   (Appendix 4)
1897 Second Edition Ordnance Survey.   (Appendix 5)

Hodgson wrote in 1832 that there had been no substantial change to Morpeth's streets since 1603, when the map for Lord Howard was made. However, if we look at these maps, we can see that the town was changing, almost as he wrote. The area behind the main streets has become a crammed-together network by 1852, getting more and more intense as the century progressed.

The three earliest maps share many features. The Wood's map and the 1853 Local Board of Health map both show a dense maze of buildings behind the front streets, but at the same time there are still many gardens close to the centre of the town. Stoney Flatts is still cultivated, plots in the angle behind Oldgate and Newgate Street are also green spaces, as is much of the land south of Oldgate and Bridge Street, and to the north east of Bridge Street.

This market town thus still had a strong link to the land-based industries, and to animals. And animals mean muck and smells, birth and death, butchery and carcasses, blood and bones.

Importantly, Morpeth's livelihood was based on its market, which had grown and flourished over the preceding centuries. By 1832, Hodgson reports that between April and Christmas, the weekly sale of oxen here was upwards of 200, and of sheep and lambs 2,500. The animals, he said, are chiefly reared and fed in Northumberland and Scotland, and consumed within the limits of the trade and ports of the Tyne and Wear. Some go as far as Leeds and Manchester, and even London.

Cattle were sold in the streets, and this continued until 1903. Old photographs show people mingling among the groups of animals, with children and women among the men. It is easy to imagine the mess, and the state of everyone's shoes and boots, especially in damp and rainy weather.

*Fig 5.1 Cattle for sale in Bridge Street, late 19th century.
Photo: K Creighton collection*

Many of the cattle would have ended their days in the back yards of Morpeth. Hodgson wrote that tanning was in former times the most staple and important trade of the town, and it was still significant in his time. The 1860 map shows three tanneries which were located behind Newgate Street towards Buller's Green, the second on the curve of the Cottingburn just north of Bridge Street, and the third to the north east of Bridge Street. All the tanneries were on the Cottingburn. There is also a tan yard and bark mill shown behind the King's Head Inn, on an 1853 drainage plan, which has become Old Tan Pits by the time of the 1860 map.

Tanning requires slaughtering and butchering. By modern standards, what went on behind the scenes in the back streets of the town in those days, turning living animals into carcasses for eating, their skins being cured so that they can be turned into pleasant and useful leather, hardly bears thinking about. It certainly went on in Morpeth.

Humans and animals lived thus in close proximity, and dealing with drains, rubbish, carcasses and effluents, in narrow crowded yards, was not easy or pleasant.

The tanning process was truly revolting.[7] The stinking process involved dealing with skins, blood, fat, flesh and hair, boiling wastes to make glue, pounding the hides, or soaking them in a slurry of dog, chicken or pigeon droppings, or human urine. We may wonder whose job it was to bring cartloads or barrels of the excrement to the tanyards, who it was that kneaded the skins with their feet, for hours at a time.

Probably it was the poorest inhabitants, including the young, who then went home to crowded rooms without the facilities to clean themselves. They would have been those who lived in the cheapest accommodation, and that would have been in the yards.

Child labour must have been a useful resource for the burgesses, who in 1843 formally requested the mayor, Wm Trotter, to "call a Public Meeting of the inhabitants of Morpeth, to take into consideration the propriety of petitioning Parliament against 'A Bill for regulating the employment of children and young persons in Factories, and for the better Education of Children in Factory districts.' "[8]

I had to read that sentence several times to be sure that they were petitioning *against* the bill to improve conditions for children. Well known Morpeth surnames appear among the fifty seven signatures, including Jobling, Matteson, Mackay, Chatto and Creighton. William Woodman, the serving clerk to the council, whose records of mid nineteenth century Morpeth are so valuable, also signed.

Other industries along the Cottingburn were a malt house, an iron foundry, a brewery, a corn mill, a saw mill, and a little further out towards the Wansbeck, a steam mill and a waulk mill. The Cottingburn had become the industrial artery of the town, and acted like an open sewer, carrying away the effluents from the various processes.

Change however was coming. In 1835, the Municipal Corporations Act had brought a new, elected council to Morpeth. The old burgesses, with their ancient links to the land, were no longer in control. The elected councillors were not necessarily owners of the original burgage plots. The modern borough council was based on election by male ratepayers.[9]

The new council, with its active town clerk William Woodman, got to grips with some of the health and hygiene problems. A death from cholera in Lumsden's Lane in Morpeth in 1848 concentrated their attention. The Public Health Act of 1849 enabled them to start attacking some of the horrific problems. One of its outcomes was the map of 1852, upon which so much of the evidence and information in this study is based. As well as this, a magnificent map, five times larger in scale than this one, was produced. It shows all the individual yards in great detail, at 120 inches, or 10 feet, to the mile. A typical yard at this scale would be about nine inches long. These maps are among our main sources of information about the yards and alleyways, and as we have seen, we are able to deduce from them street patterns which lead as far back as the early Norman period in Morpeth. They were produced as a result of a public inquiry, and as part of its recommendations.

It happened like this. The Public Health Act of 1849 allowed the new municipalities to request a government inspector to assess local conditions in a public inquiry. This would then be followed by detailed plans to be implemented by a Local Board of Health. One tenth of the inhabitants rated for the relief of the poor were required to sign their names requesting this inspection. Under the guidance of William Woodman, this was done. Of the 88 signatures, 41 had a Newgate Street address, 24 were from Bridge Street, 13 from the Market Place, five from Oldgate, and five from other individual streets. No-one with a yard address signed.

In October 1849, inspector Robert Rawlinson gave notice that he would start his examination of the witnesses. The inquiry would look into sewerage, drainage and water; burial grounds; the number and sanitary condition of the inhabitants; natural drainage; and municipal boundaries.

The "gentlemen" who were required to give evidence to the inquiry, many with familiar Morpeth names, were as follows:

Thomas King	builder
Robert Hawdon	surgeon
Matt Brumell	surgeon
Alex Bowman	painter
John Braithwaite	innkeeper
John Bates	mason
John Watson	woollen draper
John Bennett	gentleman
John Wigham	police officer
William Woodman	town clerk.

Inspector Robert Rawlinson's report was as devastating as we might expect.[10] It included a report from the Relieving Officer, William Watson, who had the job of assessing the poor in need of relief. He wrote to the inspector as follows. In the Back Riggs area, "nearly every room is occupied with paupers, many of whom have been in the receipt of relief for a great number of years, and some with both children and grandchildren … A large proportion of the illegitimate children whose mothers are natives of this town are born in them."

Rawlinson himself listed the worst areas: "Places named to me as the most unhealthy are, the north side of the Market Place, Union-street, north-east part of Oldgate; the north side of Manchester-lane, Lumsden's-lane, and Water-row."

The report stated that these poor areas had increased their population since the beginning of the 19th century, from about three thousand to four and a half thousand. This was partly owing to an influx of labourers. This was the time of the famines in Ireland, and many desperate Irish emigrants found their way to Morpeth, working on the Newcastle to Berwick railway. Many more would come seeking temporary employment during the harvest season.

Typhus was prevalent. A large number of illegitimate children were born in these dreadful yards, and more died here than in any other part of the town, from illnesses including scarlet fever, whooping cough and tuberculosis.

Rawlinson wrote: "In Lumsden's-lane I found lodging houses dirty and crowded, one of which was over a large ash-pit, the same where the woman had died of cholera. At the head of Lumsden's-yard there are also open middens and privies, the drains of which pass under the adjoining properties …

"In Union-street the houses on the east side have no yard accommodation, so that all the refuse is thrown out onto the street.

"The liquid refuse from the privies and cesspools are only removed at long and irregular intervals.

"Fever, according to medical evidence, is almost constant in these places; and cholera, as shewn, is first developed in such rooms as that over the privy and ash-pit situated in Lumsden's-lane."

There were thirty lodging houses in the town. Even for the standards of the time, those in Morpeth were shocking. They didn't necessarily have beds, and of those that did, Rawlinson wrote: "Those that offer beds have these articles of luxury filled with as many as can possibly lie upon them. Others find berths below the beds, and then the vacant spaces on the floor are occupied. Among these is a tub filled with vomit and natural evacuations."

He went on: "There is not the least discrimination of sex, but men, women and children lie indiscriminately side by side."

Those who are sensitive to such atmospheres "cannot breathe it even for a few seconds. What then must it be to those who sleep there for hours," and "the sick ward of the workhouse is filled with typhus in its worst form from these places."

The final pages of the inspector's report concludes with recommendations which should be implemented:

- a perfect system of sewers and house drains
- a full supply of pure water at high pressure
- a good surface pavement to all footwalks, passages, yards and courts
- regular cleaning of streets, courts and passages
- regulation of slaughter houses
- inspection of lodging houses, with proper separation of the sexes
- an efficient system of public lighting.

He suggests costs for these changes. He even recommends that some money could be made for selling the manure from the town, to put on the land. "At present, manure is brought by railway from Newcastle-upon-Tyne, and other places; here it may be collected from the town and can be applied to the land in the neighbourhood." He makes the case that it would be more economic to do this than to deal with the consequences of the fever.

Following this report, the Local Board of Health commissioned a set of detailed maps of the town, listed here.

1.   1852 map, scale 24 inches to the mile (Fig 1.3 and Appendix 3)
2.   1852 map, scale 120 inches to the mile
3.   1853 drainage plans, scale 120 inches to the mile.

Here is the full title of the second.

Plan of the Town
and Part of the Borough of
MORPETH
in the County of
NORTHUMBERLAND
Surveyed for the purposes of the
Health of Towns Act
VIC 11 and 12 c63 AD 1848
by
Robert Syer Hoggar
and
William Henry Rapier
Civil Engineers 1852

I have written this in detail because anyone who would like to examine the shape of Morpeth and the individual yards in 1852 will find it of the greatest interest. It is stored at Northumberland Archives, Woodhorn, and its reference is NRO 5789.

Many of the front street properties including the public houses are named. Every building in the yards behind is recorded, including the privies, stables, coach houses, slaughter houses and pigsties.

The main sewers come down Newgate Street and Oldgate, join in the Market Place, and then go along Bridge Street, past the mill sited where St George's Church is now, and then to the outflow in the Wansbeck.

What is described as the Old Water Pant goes along in parallel. This is presumably the water supply for the town, based on the reservoir on Allery Banks. In his report, Rawlinson pointed out that "Mr Thomas King constructed waterworks in 1820, with a three inch pipe which carries the water across the river to the town where it is distributed to a portion of the inhabitants only." One hundred and fifty out of 422 houses were supplied with water.

He wrote that for those with no supply: "It frequently occurs that no water can be had from the taps above the Market Place."

The third of the sets of maps are the drainage plans, as they were called. They were produced on the same scale as the second map, and included the most thorough survey of the owners and occupiers of the yards. They are thus useful as a source of much more information than the recommended drainage systems. We can learn where and what the buildings were, who lived in them and who owned them, how crowded together they were, and the locations of all the alleyways into the yards. Based on them, in the next chapter, we'll look closely at a selection of these plans.

One aspect of life in Morpeth which they reveal is the number of public houses with stables in the yards behind them. Being on the main route between Newcastle and Edinburgh, Morpeth had been one of the most important overnight stops for coaches and horses until the arrival of the railway in 1847. James Fergusson describes the excitement they used to cause. "The arrival of the four-in-hand mail and stage coaches were great events which occurred everyday, and interested almost everybody. Great passengers, the nobility and gentry, travelled in their family coaches with great state and equipage. When the Duke of Northumberland passed to, or returned from, London, there was great excitement. The Queen's Head daily, at that time, was the scene of the liveliest bustle and animation."[11]

When the post coaches were replaced by rail along the main line between London, Newcastle and Edinburgh in 1847, horse drawn carriages and carts were still essential to serve the surrounding towns and villages. Life in the many of Morpeth's yards and alleyways in the mid nineteenth century is a story of people and horses living close together.

This table summarises the services which set off from public houses, as advertised in Kelly's Directory of Northumberland, 1858. A few others stated that they set off from the main streets, but the great majority were based at inns or public houses.

Earl Grey Bridge Street	Newcastle	six every Wednesday, three each way
	Horton	Wednesday
	Whalton	Wednesday
	Rothbury	Friday
	Netherton	Friday
George and Dragon Bridge Street	Bedlington	Wednesday
Turk's Head Bridge Street	Bedlington	Monday
	Blyth	Monday
	Elsdon	Monday
	Shields	Wednesday
	Otterburn	day not stated
Fox and Hounds Newgate Street	Middleton	Wednesday
	Whalton	Wednesday
Packhorse Newgate Street	Snitter	Monday
	Shields	Tuesday, two services
	Longhorsley	Wednesday
	Longframlington	Wednesday
	Alnwick	Saturday
Lord Hood Newgate Street	Cambois	Monday to Saturday

Fig 5.2 Horse and cart carrier services from Morpeth's public houses to towns and villages in Northumberland and Tyneside

As with the cattle and other domestic animals, horses were part of the market town atmosphere, its smells, its straw and manure and mess, and its need for decent drainage.

By the time Wilson wrote his second edition of his Handbook to Morpeth, in 1884, he is able to state that "the sanitary condition of the town has much improved since the establishment of the Board (the Local Board of Health), but there is still room for improvement in the supply of water and in the lighting of the streets". [12]

If we now look at the 1897 second edition ordnance survey map, Appendix 5, we can see more and more buildings along the lengths of the yards. Stoney Flatts are built on, as are the Northfield Lands. By this time, the tan yards have gone. In 1852, the largest one closed. The industry was in decline. By the 1870s, they had all gone, "victims of a failure to modernise and of competition from Leeds."[13]

Wansbeck Iron Works is providing employment on the former Stoney Flatts. Residential areas have been built on the old Northfield Lands, the detached houses of de Merley Road and King Street, and the more modest houses of Hood Street and South Terrace. As for the yards, the rows of buildings have become lengthened and more dense. They are at their most intense by this time, and remain in a similar state until the next map, the Ordnance Survey third edition of 1922, Appendix 6. The slum clearance programmes of the twentieth century would be based on the existing pattern largely established by this date.

On the 1922 map, the addition of Pretoria Avenue has become a significant new feature. The building of this street in 1900 has preserved for posterity the curve of the ancient ploughed strips, the work of the ploughmen. Whereas other curved yards to the south of Bridge Street would be largely demolished later, the houses on Pretoria Avenue are a permanent feature, which is very fortunate.

Fig 5.3 The curved wall on this late 19th century photo is approximately the location of Pretoria Avenue, which was built in 1900. The gardens have retained the curves of the ancient ploughed strips.
Photo: K Creighton collection

Thus, in the historic town centre of Morpeth, at the end of the nineteenth century and into the first decades of the twentieth, we had a pattern of yards and alleyways behind the front streets, based on the 600 year old strips of the ploughmen, and the original tofts laid out by the de Merlays. The pattern had been concentrated further with a maze of narrow streets by the mid-nineteenth century, in the former Back Riggs, which were also ploughlands of the past.

The unsanitary nature of much of this historic network resulted in it being pulled down during slum clearance plans in the 20th century. Only bits and pieces of it would remain, almost by chance, to the present day. With our 21st century awareness, would we have permitted such clearances of historic places, slums or not, to be destroyed? Wouldn't we have wanted to save them, and improve them?

6   Down in the yards

- Queen's Head to the Earl Grey
- Lumsden's Lane
- Old Bakehouse Yard and the Millennium Green

I've chosen three sets of yards to look at in detail. They are firstly, a set of five public houses adjoining the town hall; secondly, the notorious Lumsden's Lane area where the cholera death occurred; and thirdly the yards around the Old Bakehouse Millennium Green.

The drainage plans of 1853 are the greatest source of information.[1] Each individual plan scrupulously outlines the buildings, and lists the owners and occupiers. I've cut out the individual plans, and pasted them together, in the three groups mentioned. Some of the details in the cut-outs I have added by hand. They have been taken from the 1852 large scale map, which shows further uses of the various buildings,[2] and the Morpeth land valuations book of 1910 with its associated maps.[3] Also, the individual yard plans list the names of the owners and occupiers, which I could not show in the cutouts.

It is also possible to see here the historic link between the yard plans, the ploughed oxen rigs, and the laying out of the tofts by the de Merlays borough in the thirteenth century. The width of the individual yards, despite the passing of the centuries, still relates well to the 22 yards of the ploughed acres, and this can be seen on the scales.

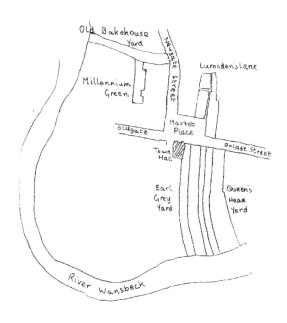

Fig 6.1 Location of three sets of yards

53

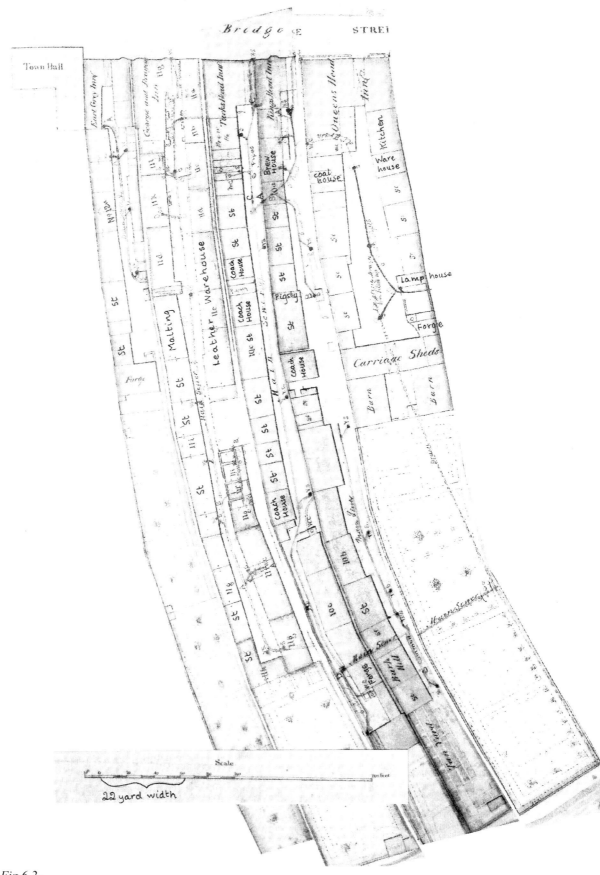

Fig 6.2₁

Queen's Head to the Earl Grey

Fig 6.3
This photo from the late nineteenth century shows the group of five inns. From the far left, part of the Queen's Head, the low building of the King's Head, the Turk's Head, a building with yard entrance leading behind the George and Dragon, which it adjoins, the Earl Grey, and then the Town Hall.
Photo: Keith Creighton collection

This group of five inns runs between the Queen's Head and the Town Hall. In 1847, the railway had replaced the post stages on the Newcastle to Berwick route, but the drainage plan surveyors drew what they saw, and so stables, coach houses and forges are very much in evidence in the yards. As we have seen in the previous chapter, numerous carriers still operated from the inns. All the yards have a series of small sheds, which would include privies and coalsheds. There are also long narrow buildings at least some of which are pigsties.

We'll start with the Queen's Head. Fergusson wrote that before the railway replaced the stage coaches in 1847, "… the Queen's Head daily at that time was the scene of the liveliest bustle and animation."4 On the plan, a large open yard behind the inn is lined with stables, with a special lamphouse, carriage sheds at the end, and barns behind. It has its own forge too. This property in 1853 is listed as belonging to one owner, Mr Andrew Lawrie, and has one occupier, presumably the innkeeper, John Braithwaite. Unlike the adjoining yards, it seems to be an inn without housing behind. Beyond the barns are gardens leading to the River Wansbeck.

Next in direction towards the Town Hall comes the King's Head Inn. It has a brewhouse directly behind the inn. The yard here is long and narrow, half the width of that of the Queen's Head. It has a long line of buildings, and at the end there is a tan yard. Thus, right in the heart of the town, we find this smelly, unhealthy operation taking place. The tan yard adjoins the Wansbeck, so the effluents would run out into the river.

The plans do not tell us whether or not it is still operating, but by 1860, at the time of the first edition ordnance survey map, this site is marked as the Old Tan Pits.

There are five stables, and a bark mill, part of the tanning operation. One building near the street is let out by Mrs Sadler to Joseph Grieve, so perhaps he was the innkeeper. There is a brewhouse directly behind the inn. Mr Robert Vinning rents out the remainder of the buildings. He has eight tenants, four of whom are women. Many are stables, but others are not named on the large 1852 map, and so may be dwellings.

After that we come to the Turk's Head. Immediately behind the inn is a brew house, a line of at least seven stables and two coach houses, and at the very end there is a forge. Mrs Ann Lewins owns three buildings just before the forge, with ten listed occupiers, four of whom are women. Mary Lewins and Richard Lewins are among them. Once again, these are the named occupiers, and it is probable that many other people shared the accommodation. This yard must have been a hive of activity.

Next comes the George and Dragon. This yard like the previous two has a long row of properties, but in this case they are on both sides of a narrow alley, facing each other. This is a yard of eleven owners, with two occupiers listed for each owner. The houses are likely to be those closest to the main street, with another cluster at the end. We can deduce this from the location of three water closets near the public house, and a couple further down the yard. Additional information from the large scale map allows us to add a malting house, four stables and a leather warehouse. Thus, behind the George and Dragon inn we find a mixture of workshops, and accommodation for people and horses.

Finally, we come to the Earl Grey. There is the usual coach-width entrance to the yard, with various buildings and a forge at the end. Mrs Ann Walker seems to own the entire property, but she has seven occupiers. As we have seen in the 1858 Kelly's directory, the Earl Grey was a great base for carriers, to and from Morpeth. The occupiers are named as James Morris, William Hunter, Geo. Taylor, Geo. Brady, Patrick Murfy, Mary Tucker and Patrick Carlington, several showing their Irish origin. Some may have lived here, with others using the buildings for their horses. There is a series of small sheds. There would have been regular comings and goings to the blacksmith, and beyond that is a series of gardens which lead down to the river.

We can deduce a little more of the history of these five yards, before they were truncated in the mid-twentieth century, from the Land Valuation Books of 1910 and their accompanying maps. From them we can see more clearly the use to which the different buildings were put. By this time, the early twentieth century, more people are living in the yards, and thus many of the stables must have been converted into, or rebuilt as, dwelling places. In this book, the Queen's Head is listed simply as a public house and stabling.

By 1910, the long narrow King's Head yard now contains almost entirely dwelling places, two of which are listed as tenements. There is a house and a workshop on the site of the Old Tan Pits. Similarly, the Turk's Head yard contains roughly half houses and half warehouses.

The wider George and Dragon yard has houses directly behind the inn, on both sides. It also contains two public houses called the Vaults and the Boar's Head. There are stables and sheds, a harness room, a granary, a byre and a chopping house. I can only guess what was chopped there. Three of the 14 dwellings are listed as tenements. Thus in 1910, this yard was still a crowded, busy hive of activity, where the needs of daily life and earning a living were side by side, the clothes washing and cooking among the coming and going of the horses and wagons.

By 1910, the Earl Grey is listed in the Land Valuations Book as a house and a shop, not at that time an inn. However, a carrier still leaves there every Wednesday for Felton, according to Kelly's Northumberland directory of 1910. None of the other four inns in this group are providing carrier services any more, although some still leave from the Grey Nag's Head and the Grey Bull, elsewhere in the town centre. Housing seems to have become the priority. Perhaps rent was the best source of income for the owners.

Kelly's directory of 1936 lists no horse drawn carriers. They have completely disappeared.

There is one poor-quality but nevertheless rare photograph which survives from this group of yards, before their demolition. It is of the George and Dragon yard, taken from Fred Moffat's booklet, Millennium, a Thousand Years of Morpeth, and may date from the 1920s or 1930s.

The photo shows a long curving yard, with steps up to the doors, and with residents rather than people at work, houses more than stables. Despite its probable twentieth century date, the layout of the buildings is likely to be close to those of 1853. The 1910 valuations showed many dwellings in this yard, particularly along the western side of the yard, as in this photo.

There will not be many people living now who remember this yard, as it was truncated prior to the development of the new flats in Baysland in the 1930s.

The photo shows the curve of the oxen rigs, just as do the drainage plans. The children in the picture are playing without the least awareness that, seven hundred years before their time, they are running and jumping in the footsteps of the ploughmen and their teams of oxen.

Fig 6.4
George and Dragon yard
in the early twentieth
century.
Photo: Alex Tweddle
collection

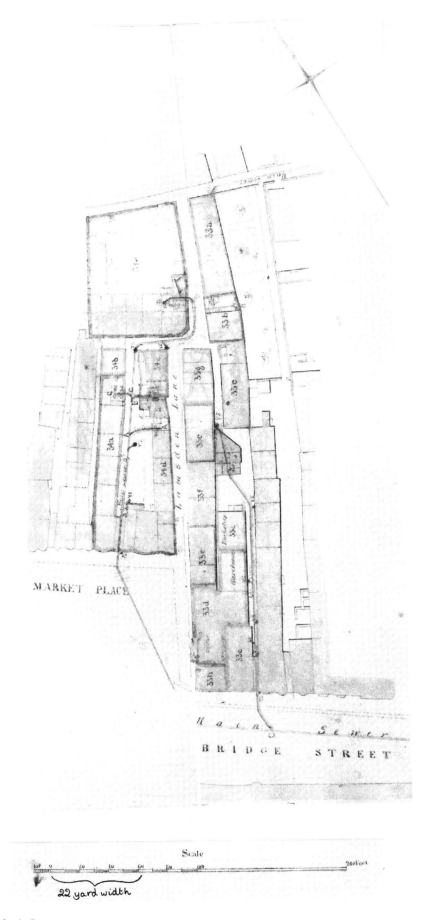

Fig 6.5 Lumsden's Lane₁

Lumsden's Lane

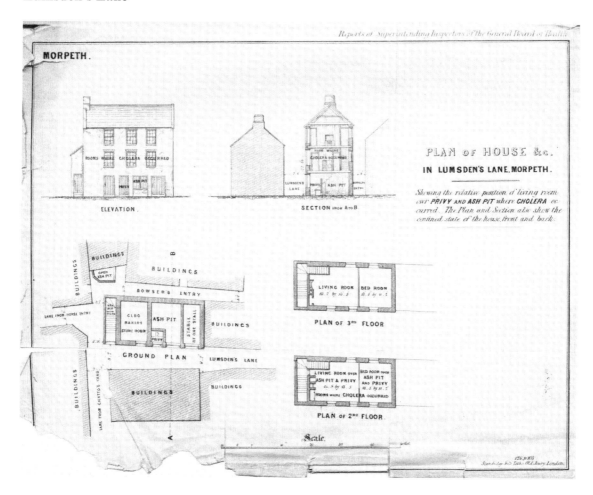

Fig 6.6
The notorious Lumsden's Lane. This plan is from Inspector Rawlinson's report of 1849.₅ The lower half of the drawing needs to be rotated 45 degrees to match the cut-outs in Fig 6.5.
Courtesy of the Society of Antiquaries of Newcastle upon Tyne.

We can see from the attached plan exactly how crowded and disgusting was the accommodation in Lumsden's Lane. The living room and tiny bedroom where the cholera death occured were on the second floor of the plan, directly over the ash pit and the privy.

The 1853 drainage plan for Lumsden's Lane was number 33. This house is numbered as 33g. Mary Lumsden lived in number 33e, at the entrance to the lane. She has the dubious fame of being part-owner of this slum property, and the lane remains named after her and her family to this day. The occupiers of 33g in 1853 were Martin Welsh, Andrew Craughlin, James Anderson and Matthew Phillips. Two of these names have an Irish ring, and one a Scottish. It is highly likely that women and children also lived in these rooms, but they remain invisible other than to our imaginations.

On the other side of Lumsden's Lane is another cluster of houses, with an enclosed yard behind it. Geo. Challoner was the owner of 34a, and he had five tenants including Jane Challoner. James Trotter and Edward Phaup owned 34b, and John Anderson was the occupier. William Creighton owned 34c. It was occupied by Robert Saddler. John Hodgson owned 34d, and he had nine tenants, among them two women, Sarah Allen and Dinah Dixon.

Finally, the cluster of properties at 34e was owned by Geo. Dodds and Others, and they had eight occupiers, three of whom were women.

We can see how narrow the alleys were from the accompanying scale. By comparison, the yards of the inns we have seen before were airy and spacious. The entrance to Lumsden's Lane is about twelve feet, and the narrower alleys to the left appear to be less than six feet wide in stretches. It would have been a great place for hide and seek, but that is about its only virtue.

In the plan from the Rawlinson report, there appear to be entrances from Chatto's Yard and Bowser's Entry, but the drainage plans do not show any access from the main streets, which are normally indicated by a cross. The whole area of housing was confined and enclosed, and going back there after a day's work, if you were lucky enough to have any, must have been like crawling back into a rat-infested warren. Perhaps if you had come from the famines of Ireland, even this was better than starving.

Old Bakehouse Yard and the Millennium Green

"So why is it called Old Bakehouse Yard?" Visitors to the Old Bakehouse Millennium Green are always asking this, and as I live there, I too have asked and tried to answer this question. The answer takes us back a long way in history.

The Norman barons required the burgesses and their wives to bake in their private bakehouses, and the de Merlays were no exception. When granting privileges in his 1239 charter to his burgesses, Roger de Merlay lll had retained various rights. The obligations on the people included payments of one in every thirteen portions of flour ground at his mill, and the baking of their bread in his *pistrina*, or bakehouse.[6]

The women of the town were supposed to bake their bread only in the lord's bakehouse. They had to pay a fee for this, and women who were lucky enough to have their own oven must have been tempted over and over again, to break this law.

Throughout the annals in Hodgson's history, we find various mentions of the bakehouse and its burgesses. The references can be found by the dates in the annals. In 1296, Henry of the Bakehouse, de Pistrina, is mentioned as a landowner. In 1312, a piece of land is exchanged, one side of which borders on the lord's bakehouse. In 1331, the boundaries of land being exchanged are "near the common bakehouse, to the water of Wanspick". In 1361, A. Backhous receives a rood of borough land in Newgate. In 1373, John Baker testified a document.

In 1380, Alan Bakhouse is noted as a bailiff. In 1381, Andrew de Bakhous was another bailiff who witnessed a land transaction. In 1398, Alan del Bakhouse is mentioned as a landholder on the north side of Hilgate, probably over on the south side of the river. The de Bakhous family, however their name is spelled, seem to be well-established townspeople.

The next mention in the annals leaps to 1663, when among the persons presented at the court leet were those who had committed the crime of "baking from the lord's common bakehouse".[7] This is described more fully in chapter 4.

After these mentions, we find no more about the bakehouse in Hodgson. We do not know where it was located in the early days. Historian Peter Tyson writes that the toll booth, on the site of the present Town Hall in the Market Place, was "probably on the same site as the manorial bakehouse", but gives no source for this statement.[8]

But why is it called *Old Bakehouse Yard?* Was there a bakehouse there? After 1663, there are a few uncertain leads towards the answer to this question.

Tweddle says that in about 1815 a route led from Newgate Street through the present day Old Bakehouse Yard to the Wansbeck, and then to the stepping stones. By 1835, this route had closed, and access to the stones was through Wigham's Yard and Main's Terrace.[9]

We can see Bakehouse Yard named as such on the Local Board of Health map of 1852, in its present location (Appendix 3). Whether it was a common bakehouse in the medieval sense, or a bakery, we are left to guess.

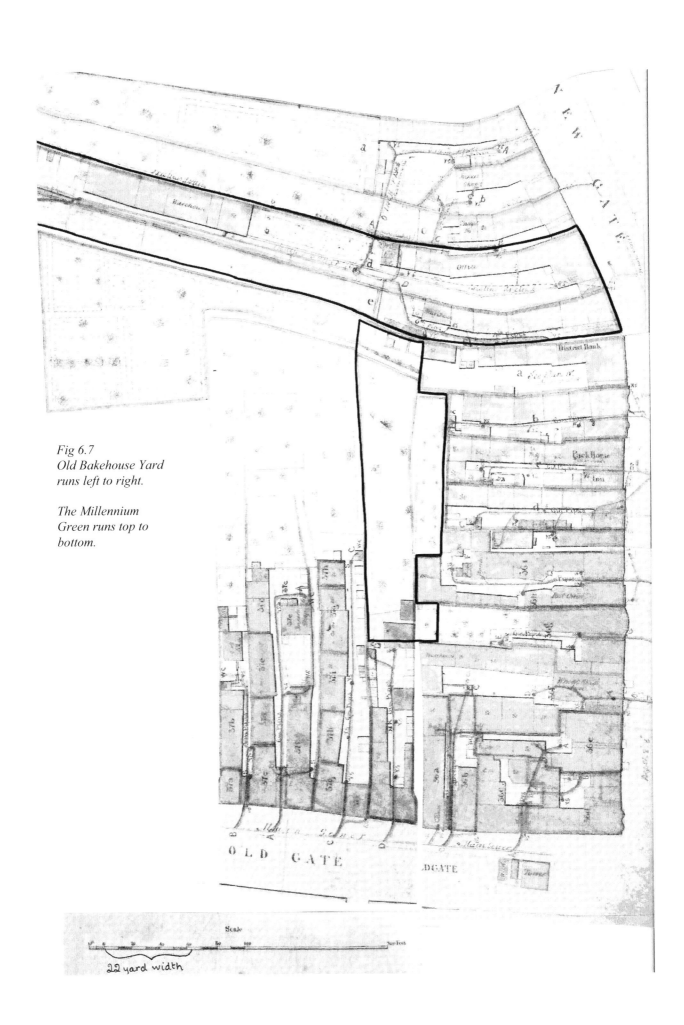

Fig 6.7
Old Bakehouse Yard
runs left to right.

The Millennium
Green runs top to
bottom.

22 yard width

62

Even into the twentieth century, people who didn't have ovens would take their dough in tins to a public bakehouse, and pay a half penny for their bread to be baked.[10] Mrs Ann Simester ran one in the Old Gaol Yard, on Bridge Street, which was recorded in the 1858 Kelly's directory of Northumberland.

In the 1897 directory, Ann Simester's bakery has gone. By this time, Mrs Margaret Kirkup was a baker at 31 Newgate Street. This is close to the present 29 Newgate Street, which is the front street property of Old Bakehouse Yard. Was her business descended from the one in 1852 which baked down the yard?

Another clue can be found on the 1860 map. (See Appendix 4.) The well known Morpeth stepping stones are marked as the Bakehouse Steps, and lead to Wigham's Yard, off Newgate Street.

The Duncans were a prominent family of bakers further up the street, at number 51. Perhaps the Bakehouse Steps led there. Once through Wigham's Yard, a short turn left would take you to their shop. They appear in the 1858 Kelly's directory, and again in 1879, 1897 and 1938. Duncan's bakery is still remembered in Morpeth, and one of the yards is named after the family.

We need to quash a rumour here, which is that ovens from the old bakery are found in the cellars of 29 Newgate Street, and hence the name Bakehouse Yard.[11] The structures have been examined by members of the Traditional Architecture Group from Newcastle. They are not ovens, but "typical wine storage bins of the sort that rather smart houses of the 18th or 19th centuries had. The cellar probably belonged to the fine 18th century house on the front street."[12]

We can see on the 1853 drainage plan that Bakehouse Yard belonged to the Earl of Carlisle, although the yards surrounding it belonged to other independent townspeople. It was an oddment, a relic dating back to his predecessors, the de Merlays, one last yard based on the oxen rigs, which he had retained, and which he was soon to sell.

The buildings on the 1853 plan were replaced in the later nineteenth century by the present terrace. By 1903, they were owned by Lloyd's Bank, of 29 Newgate Street. In 1905, Lloyd's Bank sold to William Webb, solicitor "all that dwellinghouse land and premises commonly called the Bakehouse Yard", as recorded in the deeds of my house. Thus, the name was the accustomed one, but there is no mention of any baking taking place this time.

By 1968, the house at the end of the yard, number seven, was sold to Mary Valdemar Lothian, and by this time, the name has changed to *Old* Bakehouse Yard. And thus it has remained.

By this time the yards of Morpeth had become looked upon as places where one wouldn't choose to live, as we'll see in the next chapter. The name *yard* implied slum. Hence Old Bakehouse Yard became familiarly known as Webbs' Cottages, after the owners of the big house on Newgate Street, to avoid the indignity of the residents from having to claim a disliked address.

The Webb family sold the cottages one by one, mainly during the 1970s, one last one hanging on until the nineties. But these houses were clearly no longer in slum areas. People chose to live in them, and their value was increasing.

Old Bakehouse Yard was, as we know, part of the network of old burgage plots. Land there had been compulsorily purchased by the borough council in the late sixties to provide a service road for the shops in Newgate Street. Thus it became an abandoned, unloved wilderness. There was a vegetable garden in part of it, and cars and vans parked in there, unofficially. There area was an adventure playground for my children, who called it *the alley*. My daughter Laura wrote: "You could find purple plums, blackberries, raspberries, and elderberries down the alley, if you knew where to look. The tree from which the swing hung was a place to hide and be aloof from the world. And I never did know why there lay the remains of an old mini car deeply rusted beneath all the brambles."

It became decrepit over the years though, and our children had left home. People used it as a dogs' toilet, and broken televisions were dumped among the brambles. The Old Bakehouse Community Group established the Millennium Green in 2000, with grant aid from many organisations, principally the Countryside Agency, but also Morpeth Town Council, Castle Morpeth Borough Council, BASS and the Co-op.

It can be seen clearly on the cut-out, Fig 6.7, that the Millennium Green is on the site of a former burgage plot. It leads from the rear of 14 Oldgate, behind Avril's Hairdresser and Oldgate Gallery, although it is now separated from them. The relic of a hawthorn hedge that runs through it marks an ancient boundary. Thus the Millennium Green can claim to be on one of the oldest burgage plots in the town. It is preserving a garden area which was there from at least the charter of Roger de Merlay lll in 1239, or even possibly as early as the time of Roger de Merlay l, around the date of our first created map in 1160, Fig 1.1.

So when visitors to the Millennium Green ask *But where does the name come from?* this is its story.

Fig 6.8
Old Bakehouse Yard, December 2010.

64

The era of animals and people living close together, in tight and narrow yards, is drawing to a close by the 1920s and 1930s. The period of demolition and the building of new estates on the outskirts of the town is beginning.

It is a transition period however, and in 1938, just before the outbreak of the Second World War, Kelly's directory for Northumberland still shows activity and small businesses in the yards of Morpeth. Some of these names and businesses will be resonant to people today.

Bates, Robert	smith	Back Riggs
Blackburn, Joseph	shoe repairer	Bell's Yard
Boutflower, Geo.	general smith	Corporation Yard
Caisley, Geo.	coal dealer	Whalebone Yard
Jackson, Geo.	common lodgings	Back Riggs
Jobling, Joseph	wine and spirit merchant	George and Dragon Yard
Milford and Walker	painters	Bell's Yard
Pickering, Jn	shopkeeper	7 Union Place
Varley, Arth	shopkeeper	Back Riggs
Walter Rt Beadnell	carpenter	Whalebone Yard
Warburton, Rt Maurice	boot repairer	Old Post Office Yard
Waterston, Margt Jane	servants' registry office	off Market Place
Watson, James	smith	Back Riggs

Businesses were mainly focussed on the three main streets of Bridge Street, Newgate Street and Oldgate, with the yards behind, as always. The cattle market was still an important part of town centre life. It was moved from its historic situation in front of the Town Hall to the Newmarket in 1903, gaining access through Grey's Yard in Oldgate. In the 1920s, the Scotch Arms inn adjoining the Town Hall to the west was removed, creating an opening direct to the market. It was not until 1957 that a new mart was opened on Stobhill.

In the meantime, the cattle were guided down to the town centre from the railway station. The muck, mess and animal life had not left the town centre yet. Eddie Purdy worked in Bobby Rutherford's barber shop in Bridge Street. "There were cattle pens in the new Market Place then, by the river. The Irish men brought the cattle from Ireland, and the *bull wallopers* brought them down from the station through the street. Everyone put shutters on the shop windows so the cattle wouldn't break the glass. The Irish men came in to get a shave in our shop, and they did their business there. When they completed a bargain, they put a silver coin on their palm, and spat on it, and slapped each other's palm to seal the transaction. They felt really foreign to us. They were hard working, hard drinking men."

He said: "We used to call market day the cock and hen day. All the farmers' wives would bring their hens and eggs and sell them in the Town Hall. Yes, right inside, in the main part of the hall."

Despite the public inquiry and recommendations by Rawlinson in 1849, the condition of housing in the yards did not seem to be much changed.

Dorothy Robson was a Labour councillor in the 1930s. She blamed the landlords for the decay of the properties. In her autobiography she wrote about "the criminal neglect of the local authority to supply reasonable sanitation and to compel landlords to toe the line, but as many of the councillors were the slum owners, drawing good rents without spending anything on the property, what could we expect?"[1]

She continued: "More than two thirds of the people living in the borough had no water indoors, and only earth closets. When we urged 'privy conversion', we were told it was not in the interests of the town, whose main industries were agriculture and market gardens, and needed the contents of the middens to put on the land."

There is more. "Most authorities who had earth closets arranged for the cleaning out to be done by night, but not Morpeth Borough. The evil smelling filth was shovelled out of the middens into an open cart. I have seen the baker's van, butcher's van, green grocer's flat cart and the midden cart in close close proximity in the back lane. On windy days it was common to see pieces of paper covered with excrement blowing about. I once saw a piece adhere to a child's face."

In 1935, she was asked to give evidence to a public inquiry. She describes one of many visits to the yards behind Bridge Street. "I used to call it Dicken's World. The tenements behind Bell's Yard were very broken down, six storeys high, but only five could be used because there was no roof. Slates had broken away, pigeons nested there, and the filth was over two feet deep. Each tenement consisted of only one large room, with a small window, and an old fashioned fireplace with oven and boiler. All the families were large. We went into one room on the fifth floor. Husband, wife and children ate, slept, bathed, did everything in that one room." Due to the pigeon filth above, the ceiling was discoloured and sagging, and the occupier who was a pitman, had propped it up with batons.

On the other side of the narrow street were earth closets, one for every five families. Conditions were similar in Forrest Yard, a little further along Bridge Street. "We asked to see the toilets, and were taken to a brick building of earth closets, one to accommodate 32 people. The wooden seats had two holes, so that two persons could use them at the same time. Hinges were off the doors so privacy was not possible. The closets had not been cleaned out for some time and human filth was higher than the holes. One must stand on the seat, astride the holes if one must use it."

Outside this building was the tap where residents drew drinking water. There was a grate under the tap, and a hole in the wall near the ground, to enable the liquid substance to escape the earth closet and down the grate.

She lists: "These were only two yards. There were many more, Corporation Yard, George and Dragon Yard, Old Queen's Head Yard, Whalebone Yard, Old Bakehouse Yard, Royal Oak Yard, Granby Buildings, and many more. There was Masons Arms Yard, the one where the rats were so numerous, where a baby had been badly bitten by them."

Tweddle comments on these conditions. "Though the property here and in other yards was in appalling condition and calling out for demolition, there were in them many honest, hard-working and caring parents who struggled hard against adverse conditions to keep their children clean, tidy and in good health." Moreover in 1935, Forrest Yard was commended for being one of the best decorated areas in the town at the King George V's Silver Jubilee celebrations.[2]

Councillor Mrs Robson's autobiography was written in the 1970s, looking back on her earlier work. "Housing of the working classes was a very urgent matter. I called on the Town Clerk, who told me proudly that Morpeth was one of the first authorities to build houses for the working classes, and received high praise from the Ministry of Health. Perhaps the fact that some of the councillors were builders had something to do with that. The council was made up almost entirely of businessmen, all with an axe to grind."[3]

She noted that records in 1930 showed the following new streets of council housing:

1890	Burt Terrace area, thirty one houses
1891	Alexandra Road area, forty two houses
1919	High Stanners, seventy two houses
1923	Armstrong Terrace, forty five houses
1924	St Mary's Field, eighty four houses
1925	Wellwood Gardens, twenty four houses
1928	Duncan Gardens, forty two houses.

The flurry of slum clearances and council house building continued into the 1960s. This list continues with extractions from Tweddle's Town Trails.

1935	Baysland, fifty six flats	no 1, p11
1936 – 1937	Sanderson Gardens, fifty six houses	no 4, p13
1936 – 1937	The Avenues, Stobhill, over 100 houses	no 9, p1
1933 – 1954	Spelvit Lane	no 4, p15
1949 – 1962	Church Walk	no 10, p33

Tweddle reports that the first council houses on the High Stanners were built for those returning from the First World War, and "in an effort to solve the problems of over-crowding in the old yards and courts of the town".[4]

From 1936 to 1937, he writes that "First, Second, Fourth, Fifth, Seventh, Ninth and Tenth Avenues were built at Stobhill to accommodate some of the inhabitants of the 131 town dwellings proclaimed by the Medical Officer of Health to be unfit for human habitation – with another 32 classified as in an unsatisfactory condition."

Most of these condemned houses were in
  • George and Dragon Yard, King's Head Yard and Mill Lane - south of Bridge Street
  • Forrest Yard, Union Street, Bowser Court and Bell's Yard - north of Bridge Street
  • Royal Oak Lane (Old Bakehouse Lane) and Wigham Yard - west of Newgate Street
  • Bilton's Court, Capel Place, Flint's Buildings - east of Newgate Street
  • Manchester Street, Low Stanners and Hillgate.

Bungalows at Challoner's Gardens in the High Stanners were built in 1957 "to meet the needs of pensioners who generally prefer to live on flat land near the town centre rather than on outlying estates."

Now let's take a look at this photo taken in about 1930, before the demolitions really got going.

Fig 7.1 Morpeth in the 1930s.
Photo: Ken Stait

Only a few people can remember what it was like to live in this area. Eddie Purdy, who described market day in Morpeth earlier, is at the time of writing aged 83. He was born and grew up in the Back Riggs, in the centre right of the photo.

"I lived at 11 Granby Buildings. There was a blacksmith opposite my house. The great shire horses used to come in to be shod. The Corporation horses had a stable there. It was the far end of Mackay's Yard. The horses pulled the carts which emptied the earth privies. Next to their stable there was the midden, and it was buzzing with bluebottles in the summer.

"The area in front of my house was cleared in 1949 and 1950. They'd already cleared the house just in front of ours, Pickering's Yard, Watson's Buildings. That was where the Visoccis and Bertorellis lived. They had an ice-cream parlour on Newgate Street. They were Italian prisoners of war who stayed here after the war.

"I was born in 1928. In those days, everyone in Morpeth knew each other. They were class conscious times. There were three levels. The professionals, doctors and solicitors and so on. Then the business people, who were the shop owners. And then the ordinary working people, like us. The professionals looked down on the business people, and the business people looked down on us.

"We were not well to do, but we had a lot of self respect. We always looked after the yard, and our houses. The women would scrub the front door sill with a scrubby stone. You wet the stone, rubbed a brush on it, and then scrubbed the step. It made a nice orangey yellow colour. On Saturdays especially, my mother cleaned the house from top to bottom, until it was spotless. She was very house proud.

"My father was a miner. He worked at Howburn Pit. He died when I was six or seven, so my mother had to bring us up on her own. She had five children, but three died. One was stillborn, one died I think of pneumonia, and the other of bronchitis. She had to support us as well as she could, and she took in washing.

"First, the water had to be collected in buckets from a standpipe in the yard. She heated it in a big pan, on the black range, and then she had to pour it into the poss tub. She would thump the clothes up and down with the poss stick. When clean enough, the clothes had to be put through the big mangle and rinsed, and mangled and rinsed once or twice more. They were hung out on lines to dry, and if it was wet weather, she would put them on the clothes horse round the fire. When they were ready, she had to iron them. She heated up the flat irons by the fire. When it was all done, she would take the basket to the houses in Dacre Street and Cottingwood Lane, and she would get two shillings and sixpence for a basketful.

"She turned her hand to all sorts. She baked pies and peas, and made ginger wine. People came to the house, and she sold them at the door.

"The landlords were keen enough to collect the rents, but they didn't do anything to repair the properties, and that was why they deteriorated. We were offered a council house in 1950. We were lucky enough to get one in the High Stanners, my sister Edna, my mother and me.

"We came to a different world. We had a bathroom, electricity, indoor plumbing. We'd only had gas lights in our other house. It was a step up in our social life. But the people in the old Back Riggs were good people, respectful of authority, and our mother used to bring us up by the Bible."

It is pleasing to hear such a strong affirmation of courage. Eddie Purdy's mother was able to live the rest of her life in comfort, after the struggles of her earlier years. There is a sense of pride in the overcoming of hardships in Eddie's story.

A 1920's Monday morning
at Bullers Green.

Fig 7.2
Washing clothes at Bullers Green, Morpeth.
Drawing by Frederick Moffat, from his booklet From
Bowles Green to Bullers Green.

Returning to the photo, we can see how Bridge Street runs away to the right of the picture, Oldgate to the bottom, and Newgate Street curves away in the centre left. Union Street, as described by Hodgson, runs parallel to Newgate Street, a little higher in the photo. King Street runs off at right angles to it, to the top centre of the photo, and Dacre Street to the top left.

Most of those tightly packed houses, in the yards and alleyways have gone. In their place are car parks, Morrison and Lidl supermarkets, and the Sanderson Arcade shopping centre. Those readers who know old Morpeth will be able to identify places they used to know. Others may just be amazed at how crowded it was, and how closely together people lived.

It makes me think of places like Fez in Morocco, or Seville in southern Spain, World Heritage Sites, and the countless historic town centres in Europe and worldwide, with narrow winding streets and private corners. Often they have or had inadequate sanitation and nasty corners too. How has it happened that they have survived, while Morpeth's have been allowed to disappear? Even acknowledging that many of those properties were slums, much could have been done to improve them, and to preserve these historic patterns of settlement.

Alan Davison has this childhood memory, when he was about ten years old. "My Auntie Meggie Jane lived in Stafford's Yard, and my Uncle Jack had pigs and poultry up at Buller's Green. At Christmas time, they would kill the pigs, and we boys would go up to the yard, and there would be the pig hanging up, with its neck cut, and a bucket underneath catching all the blood for the black puddings. All the women would be there plucking the poultry, and the yard was knee deep in feathers. This would be about 1948."

Alan's aunt and uncle "took in long distance drivers for bed and breakfast, and it was always full because they had a supply of eggs and ham that were hard to get in the forties and early fifties. Uncle Jack was a blacksmith at Swinney's iron works. He used to collect the dinner waste from the schools, and boil it in Stafford's Yard in an outhouse to make pig swill. I was lucky, because I used to take boiled ham and black pudding home."

And about the notorious Back Riggs, he said: "My friends, brothers and I used to go through the lanes behind the Horse Entry, and one day the people who lived inside threw sandwiches at us out of the houses." He couldn't remember if he ate the sandwiches or not.

Jacob Conroy was one of nine children, and grew up in Manchester St, next to the Mason's Arms of rat fame in Councillor Mrs Robson's report. His mother was the cleaner for the lodging house next door. She would tell them all about the rats running around. There was one alley that was so bad it was known as Shitty Alley.

He remembered Olivers' the baker on Bridge Street. In the yard behind the shop, there was a boiler where they used to melt down fat for the bakery, and leave it overnight. His father did maintenance work there, and when he went in, in the morning, all the rats used to scamper away from the cauldron. They used the fat in the cakes, which they then sold in the shop.

Fig 7.3
Old Herald Office Yard, behind Bridge Street, 1950s.
Photo: William Wallace collection

Margaret Mackay described the Morpeth Herald Yard, behind their front street shop on Newgate Street. "When I look at that photo, I can remember it all. On the right, first is the building that became Stead and Simpson's shoe shop. I used to hit my tennis ball against that wall, and once I smashed one of the windows. It was good fun, hitting a ball against a hard brick wall. Next was Ken Rogers' workshop. He was a joiner. Beyond that Mr and Mrs Wetheral had a house, with their two daughters. That is her there, in the picture. Then, further along again, Mrs Dorothy Daglish lived. She'll be ninety now. At the end of the yard, you turned right into Granby's Buildings.

"There was Watson's blacksmiths, on the left end as you look at the picture. The horses came into the yard from the top. The Corporation kept its horses in a stable next to that. Once, one of the horses died in its stable. It was so big that it was a real job getting it out. The horses used to pull the dust carts collecting the rubbish round the town. That would be in the forties and fifties.

"This yard is the last cobbled yard of Morpeth. The cobbles are still there, under the tarmac. Someone just came and dumped it on top of them one day.

"The buildings at the top were compulsorily purchased by the borough council, to re-develop the Back Riggs area. The whole lot came down in 1971 or 72. David Hicks the furniture restorer bought some buildings that were left. He's still there.

"It was good to get rid of that dirty area. I wasn't allowed to go through there when I was a girl. It was a slum. You never knew what you would catch. It was so crowded that I couldn't imagine living in it. But that was the normal life at the time. You didn't know anything different."

By the fifties and sixties, many of the yards had gone, but there were still some empty properties waiting to be demolished. Cynthia Peverley lived on Kirkhill. "Me and my friends used to play in the derelict houses behind Newgate St, on the way back from school. It would be about 1967. We would run up and down the old stairs, playing hide and seek. We were fascinated by all the pretty wallpaper on the walls. No-one used to know we did it. It was a great place to play."

Ken Stait and Kim Bibby-Wilson both remember the big open spaces where all the houses behind Newgate and Bridge Streets had been pulled down. Ken said that when he was a little boy, he would walk with his mother down Union Street to King Street, but that most of the yards had gone by that time. Kim used to play with her friend in the early 1960s, "acting-out story games with my friend Elspeth Hamilton in what appeared to be waste land with a small or partly demolished shed area to the rear of her family's house in Dacre Street. The land seemed to be fairly open, and was behind several of the houses with no fences or walls."

I myself arrived just too late to know the old areas before demolition. One sunny August day, in the memorable hot summer of 1976, with two little boys and pushchair, I walked down Old Bakehouse Yard. I'd been given the key to number two by the estate agent. "You won't want that house," said the agent at Rickard's. "It only has one bedroom, and an outside toilet." But I wanted to look anyway, as we needed a cash purchase, and this was the cheapest house in Morpeth at the time, with an asking price of £4,500.

We went past the old brick property behind 29 Newgate Street, down a weedy green earthen lane, to a little row of stone houses. We went past the first one, which was covered with grey render, to number two, built of beautiful old golden stone. The green lawn in front was overhung by a great ash tree, and the grassy gardens and trees spread further down towards the river. It seemed like a tiny paradise. Inside we went, to a large light room, with a tiled coal fireplace. Beyond that was a small prefabricated kitchen with a roof light. Outside the kitchen door was a concreted yard with a toilet and hanging chain, open to the air, and a coal shed. We went up some wooden stairs to the single bedroom. The large window overlooked the green school playing field and the attractive church of St Robert. It was all so beautiful, and unbelievably cheap.

My husband came to see it, and was captivated too. We eventually bought the house for £4,750, and have lived there ever since. We were surprised to learn that not everyone thought it was a bargain, the yards at that time not being considered desirable places to live. There had been demolition in the yard of some houses closer to Newgate Street, but miraculously the row which included ours had survived.

In the 1970s, local authority grants were available to improve the remaining unmodernised properties in the town. The last children in Morpeth were having their baths by the fire, or braving the cold to cross the back yard to go to the toilet. Soon, everyone had an indoor bathroom, and hot and cold water.

Fig 7.4
Bathtime down the yards, 1976.
Photo: author's family album

As for what it was like to live in there, my daughter Laura writes: "I was born in the bed, in the bedroom, in the house, that is 2 Old Bakehouse Yard. There's something cosy about living down a yard. It's a place that doesn't go on forever. It's a place you can't get lost in. It's a place that keeps you safe from both sides. It's a place that you have to choose to enter through one entrance to seek your purpose there.

"I would describe Old Bakehouse Yard as a beautiful, intriguing and higgledy-piggledy kind of place. Some people had lived there for years and seen so many changes. Significant to me was the lowering of our garden wall to let the light in, and making it easier for the children to leap over it and down to the river.

"You never knew who you might bump into in Old Bakehouse Yard; mother ducks shuffling their newly hatched down to the river, visitors to the town adoring the lovely sandstone houses and sweet gardens, especially my mother's roses stretching up and across the house, some children thinking they could access the river that way, or maybe lovers who slipped off main street for a sneaky kiss. Although you couldn't smell bread being baked in Old Bakehouse Yard, you could smell your dinner cooking from the moment you turned into the archway."

We had bought our house knowing that a service road was due to run directly across the access between these houses and Newgate Street. This was officially in the local plan. The estate agent at Rickard's thought that it would never happen, and it didn't. Once again, by good luck, this part of Morpeth's historic town centre has survived.

Eventually the borough council gave its compulsorily purchased area for the development of the Millennium Green. They sold it for one pound. One day, the red-cloaked mayor wearing his golden chain accepted one penny each from the children of St Robert's school, as payment for the land.

The rash of demolitions in the yards was virtually over by the 1970s. What was left was either developed and made attractive, as with the Wheatsheaf Yard, or improved by the homeowners as in Old Bakehouse Yard, or just left in peace as in Challoner Place on Oldgate.

The former Back Riggs area was developed into a new shopping centre. It is described in Town Trail No 5 by Alec Tweddle. "The quadrangle and the surrounding two-storey red-brick buildings with red pantile roofs (in which the Co-op Supermarket with its mirror windows facing west, occupies the largest space) give an attractive Dutch appearance to this part of Morpeth." He adds: "The new Back Riggs, with its carefully landscaped car park, is by no means unpleasing to the eye."

This development too is history. It has been replaced by the new Sanderson Arcade shopping mall, which opened in November 2009.

We have now followed this journey as far as the second decade of the twenty first century. A walk along Bridge Street, Newgate Street and Oldgate on any day of the week will show people making their way to and from their destinations, using the network of alleys which remain. I decided I would do a survey of them, to see how many they are using.

The results surprised me, and seem to surprise most people I talk to.

Along the south side of Bridge Street there are six open yards and alleyways used as through routes, and one closed; along the north side there are another seven open routes and two closed.

Along the west side of Newgate Street there are three open routes leading to the Stepping Stones, and several others leading to private houses and to the Millennium Green; along the east side another five open routes are regularly used between the bus station and Newgate Street.

Along the south side of Oldgate there are two open routes and another four closed.

This makes a total of 23 through routes. It does not include the other 11 or more to which people have access but have to return the way they go in, and some which can be used but have the appearance of being private or for the use of business premises. I've mapped them out , and named them.

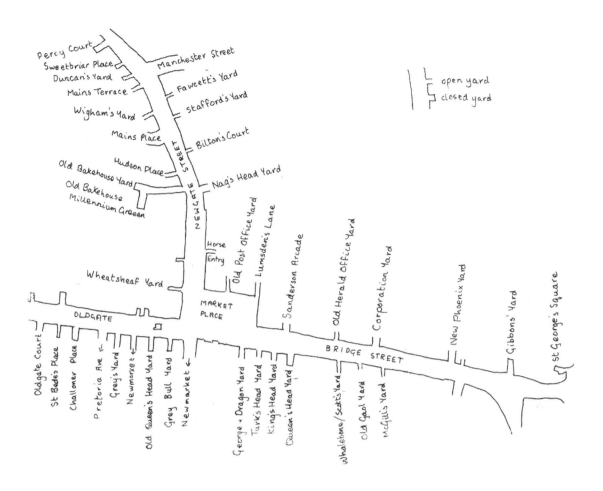

Fig 7.5
Open and closed alleyways leading to yards, from the main streets.

People are using the open alleyways, and probably assume they are rights of way, but are they? I next took a visit to County Hall, to examine the definitive rights of way map. I found out that only one of them is a right of way, and that is Wigham's Yard, leading from Newgate Street to the Stepping Stones.

When I did my survey, I also learned that at one time virtually all of the buildings on the three main streets had access to a yard at the back, either through an archway wide enough for a horse and cart, or a narrower one for individual people or animals. Except for those which can be seen on the map, the access to the yards behind has usually been incorporated into the business premises, creating extra internal space. Frequently the narrower access leads to upstairs flats or offices. There are dozens of these quiet doorways, which we walk past and barely notice. They are most easily seen on Newgate Street where the shop fronts are less modernised, but they exist on Bridge Street too.

If we follow Tweddle's Town Trails, we can find explanations for many of the names of the existing yards and alleys. Others I've found by making enquiries. They are often named after public houses which no longer exist, or previous owners of the property on the main street. Where there are gaps, perhaps readers can fill them.

1. From the town hall, along the south side of Bridge Street

George and Dragon Yard	former public house
Turk's Head Yard	former public house
King's Head Yard	former public house
Queen's Head Yard	hotel and public house
Whalebone Yard or Scott's Yard	former public house/Scott was a jeweller trading here
Old Gaol Yard	former gaol
McGill's Yard	

2. From the north side of the Market Place along Bridge Street

Old Post Office Yard	the building to the east was a post office in 1808
Lumsden's Lane	Mary Lumsden was owner and occupier of no 33 in 1853
Sanderson Arcade entrance	Alderman W.S. Sanderson, four times mayor of Morpeth
Old Herald Office Yard	Morpeth Herald office until 1983
Corporation Yard	council office 1905 – 1916
New Phoenix Yard	former public house
narrow alley name not known	
Gibbons' Yard	named after owner of garage
St George's Square	St George's church is nearby

3. From the corner of the Market Place along the west side of Newgate Street, as far as the telephone exchange

Wheatsheaf Yard	former public house
Old Bakehouse Yard	possible former 19th century bakehouse
Hudson Place	a well known Morpeth family
Mains Place	named after Mains Terrace
Wigham's Yard	
Mains Terrace	Mains was a cycle shop here, and Mains Terrace was in a yard behind
Duncan's Yard	The Duncan family were long established bakers here
Sweetbriar Yard	
Percy Court	

4. From Appleby's Bookshop, along the east side of Newgate Street and into the Market Place.

Fawcett's Yard	Benjamin Fawcett was a vet who practised here from 1868
Stafford's Yard	James Stafford was a joiner and timber merchant at nearby Wellway
Bilton's Court	Ann Bilton was the landlady of a nearby pub, the Fox and Hounds, in 1855
Nag's Head Yard	former public house
Horse Entry	an old name which appears on the 1826 map, though a little further north

5. Along the south side of Oldgate

Grey Bull Yard	former public house
Old Queen's Head Yard	former public house
Grey's Yard	a well known Morpeth family
Challoner Place	a well known Morpeth family
St Bede's Place	location of a former Catholic chapel
Oldgate Court	a new name

The yards and alleyways along the north side of Oldgate are not listed because they are not very obvious. One closed yard is accessed behind the Indian restaurant, and another alley with houses is 10A and 12 Oldgate. The former Pear Tree Yard on this street was in the area behind the Royal Mail premises.

Morpeth is luckier than many traditional market towns in that it still has a lively number of local businesses in the old main streets, even though in this twenty first century, they are struggling to survive against the competition of the supermarkets. A quick walk down the streets reveals the following small independent traders.

Along Newgate Street's west side, there are bakers and butchers, who still bake and chop to the rear of the shops, photographer, greengrocer, newsagent, hairdressers and barbers, the Morpeth Herald office where they still type up the stories, cobbler, off-licence, home decorating and art gallery. There are Indian and Chinese take-aways, another hairdresser and a second hand bookshop.

Down the east side, we find a white goods store, motor parts supplier, bookshop, beauticians, two jewellers, florist, sewing shop, giftshop, clothiers, baker and butcher, tile shop, kitchen saleroom, stationers, fish and chip shop, and a public house.

Along Market Place and the north side of Bridge Street, we find pet shop, newsagents, a public house, hairdresser, funeral director, sports clothier, and window, conservatory and carpet supplier.

On the south side of Bridge Street, are children's clothier, gift shop, the famous emporium of Smail's ironmongers, cafes, hairdresser and beautician, the great Rutherford's department store and a hotel.

In Newmarket we find a sandwich shop, shoe shop, bar, sun tan parlour, fish and chip restaurant, greengrocer and florist, delicatessen and newsagent.

Along Oldgate there are cafes, pound shop, picture framer, hairdresser, gift shop, dry cleaners, cheese shop and clothier.

Among these independent traders are sprinkled the professional services, including opticians, solicitors, estate agents, dentists, travel agents, banks, building societies and alternative therapy practitioners. There are numerous restaurants, often on the first floors. There are charity shops, but not too many.

There are many chain shops too but I haven't listed them. Newgate Street has the liveliest record of independent shops, and has its own self-help group, the Newgate Street Traders.

These independent traders are an important part of the life and soul of the town. Their premises are still sited on the historic burgage plots, with the yards behind, even though the yards have been radically truncated.

Some businesses are using the yards to advantage, in particular the public houses like the Black Bull, the White Swan and the Comrades Club. Some new businesses are set up with the yards as their front face, including a fishing supplier, whose address is 3 and 4 Fawcett's Yard, and a perfumier who uses a Newgate Street address. Old Bakehouse Yard has a thriving coffee shop and a toddlers' outfitter selling "new and lightly used" items.

Patches is a clothing repair shop, 9 and 10 Bilton's Yard. Pat Ennion, the proprietor, tells us that what is now her shop used to be two one-up-one-down houses. When she set up business in the early 1980s, an old woman who was in her nineties, came to see her. She had been born in one of the houses, and was one of nine children. The three girls slept upstairs in the parents' bedroom. The six boys slept on the landing.

One very traditional business still flourishes in the Old Morpeth Herald Yard. David Hicks' furniture restoration workshop is in one of Morpeth's oldest buildings, probably medieval, with nineteenth century alterations.5

There are many yards which used to exist, and have disappeared, some examples of which are mentioned above in Councillor Dorothy Robson's descriptions. Others lie secretly behind shop fronts, barely used, or have been developed like that behind the Black Bull. For anyone who would like more detail of their locations, I recommend Davison and Harle's version of Tweddle's Town Trail No 5.

There is thus still business life in the yards of Morpeth. Several of them now have signs facing the backs, as well as the main streets. The new shopping mall, which replaces yards behind Bridge Street, is a hub for shoppers, and has some local independent traders as well as a range of chain stores.

As for housing, there are new projects in the places where the old yards or run-down areas used to be. It is present day government policy to put housing in brownfield sites in town centres, to some extent replacing what has been demolished. These are behind Oldgate, Bridge Street and Newgate Street, and they have brought new life to the town centre. The developers adopted the old names, or devised likely sounding new ones. Thus we have Oliver's Mill, Chantry Mews, Whalebone Lane, Oldgate Court and Mains Place.

Ken Stait runs a thriving photography shop in the Market Place. He is active in the Chamber of Trade, the organisation of local businesses which has inherited the role of the old burgesses. He looks back on what has gone with mixed feelings. "The people who lived in the old yards and the Back Riggs wanted modern conveniences. It was so much easier to live in a new house, with your own kitchen, and a garden. You could take a bus or drive to the town centre from the estates to do your shopping. In those days, no-one thought about what it would do to the town. It used to be dead, empty, in the evenings here. There are more people living here now with the new buildings, and it is more lively."

He continued: "But the demolitions went too far. The old Sanderson's brewery was the last decent-sized semi-industrial building, in the old Back Riggs. It lay empty in the seventies. When you went in, you could see the old iron beams. It still had a roof. It should have been preserved, like Oliver's Mill, and made into flats. And what is in its place? That low-rise flat-box-pack of Lidl."

Morpeth is still a market town. Every Wednesday, the market takes place on its eight hundred year old site, and the farmers' market comes once a month. The Sanderson Arcade occupies the site between the former Bell's Yard, Bowser's Entry and Lumsden's Lane. The supermarkets on the old Stoney Flatts and Back Riggs compete for customers, while new ones battle for sites on the Low Stanners and the outskirts of the town.

It is a surprising little town. Somehow, it has hung on to its traditions, its feisty Chamber of Trade, its own local newspaper, its own town council with a mayor, and its family-owned shops where you can buy much of what you need without using a supermarket. The shops on the tofts, on the ancient burgage plots; the network of alleyways linking them, and the secretive yards behind; they are all deeply connected with the past, while they serve the needs of the present day. It is an inheritance from long ago, which we may not think about as we rush around on our errands. Because of this, I have wanted to draw attention to an aspect of the history of our old town, just to remind us of what we have, and what we could value more.

Let us finish with a view from Haw Hill, with a photo which was taken in the early years of the twentieth century. We are standing on the top of the mound, as the de Merlay barons did, looking down at the prize they had won in the conquest, watching the ox teams working the fertile land on the other side of the river. We are looking at the crowded buildings, where people lived and worked through the middle ages. It was the skill of the ploughmen who formed the curving rigs, and the decision of the barons to lay out the town on those lines, that formed the patterns we see. Over the centuries, we have learned about ploughmen and burgesses; guild members and shopkeepers; marketers and modern day shoppers; all those people then and now, who have made their way through the old yards and alleyways of Morpeth.

Chapter notes

Chapter 1   **It all started with the ploughmen**

1 John Hodgson   p 115
    William Kapelle   p 193
2 S R Eyre   p 86
3 C S Orwin   p 34
4   "   p 36
5 R Adkins   p 417
6 C S Orwin   pp 32-33
7 A H Tweddle no 8   p19
8 John Hodgson   p 58

Chapter 2   **Houses on furrows**

1 John Hodgson   pp 10-11, p 56
2   "   p 11
3   "   p 11
4   "   p 57
5   "   p117
6   "   p 58
7 James Finlayson   p 20
8 John Hodgson   p 11
9 James Finlayson   pp 13-14
10 John Hodgson   p117
11 Mark Bailey   p 246
12 John Hodgson   p 118
13   "   p 118
14   "   p 58
15   "   p 119 onward

Chapter 3   **Foreigners rule the town**

1 John Hodgson   p 10
    Percy Hedley   p 197
2 Melvyn Bragg   p 56
3 William Kapelle   p 194
4 Percy Hedley   p 196
    John Hodgson   p 115
5   "   pp10-13
6 Maurice Beresford   p26 English Medieval Boroughs
7 Maurice Beresford   p 9 New Towns of the Middle Ages
8   "   pp 208 – 209   "
9   "   pp 191 – 197   "
10   "   p 59   "

Chapter 4   **Burgesses amid the conflicts**

1 John Hodgson   p 64
2 Richard Lomas   p 37
3   "   p 38
4   "   pp 44 - 48
5   "   pp 3 - 68
6 Roland Bibby   p 8
7   "   p 7

8	"		p 12
9	John Hodgson		p 46 – 47
10	A H Tweddle	no 10	p 29
11	Geoffrey Watson		p 47
12	A H Tweddle	no 4	p5
13	John Hodgson		p167
	en.wikipedia.org/wiki/Margaret_Tudor		
14	A H Tweddle	no 4	p 5
15	Roland Bibby		various
16	A H Tweddle	no 4	p 6
17	"	no 4	pp 7 - 8
18	Bridget Gubbins travel journal		
19	Leo Gooch		pp61-74

Chapter 5   **Slums on the riggs**

1	R Rawlinson	p259, then p12
2	R Rawlinson	p259, then p27
3	Ian Willis	p 81
4	"	p 81
5	"	p 85
6	Morpeth Collectanea ll	p 35
7	Alan Davison AHT no 5	addendum
8	Morpeth Collect. IV	p134
9	Roland Bibby	p 27
10	R Rawlinson	p 259, then pp 1-54
11	James Fergusson	p 18
12	Wilson	p 14 - 16
13	Ian Willis	p 78

Chapter 6   **Down in the yards**

1	Drainage plans	NRO 5445
2	Map	NRO 5789
3	Land valuations & map	NRO 436/64
4	James Fergusson	p 18
5	R Rawlinson	p 262
6	John Hodgson	p 119
7	"	p 155
8	P Tyson	p189
9	A H Tweddle no 3	p 13
10	Dorothy Robson	p 151
11	A H Tweddle no 2	p 3
12	Margaret Maddison	email to author

Chapter 7   **Heritage from the ploughmen**

1	Dorothy Robson	pp 417 - 419
2	A H Tweddle no 5	p 10
3	Dorothy Robson	p 409 and 128
4	A H Tweddle no 3	p 12
5	www.keystothepast.info	

Bibliography

Adkins, R, Adkins, L, and Leitch, V, *The Handbook of British Archaeology*, Constable, 2008

Bailey, Mark, *The English Manor,* Manchester University Press, 2002

Beckensall, Stan, *Place Names and Field Names of Northumberland,* Tempus, 2006

Beckett, John, *England's Last Open Field Village*, trustees of Laxton Visitors Centre, 1989

Beresford, Maurice, *New Towns of the Middle Ages*, Lutterworth Press, 1967

Beresford, Maurice, *English Medieval Boroughs,* 1973

Bibby, Roland, *The Medieval Guilds of Morpeth,* Morpeth Antiquarian Society, 1998

Bogle, Kenneth, *Scotland's Commons Ridings*, Tempus, 2004

Bragg, Melvyn, *The Adventure of English,* Hodder & Stoughton, 2003

Cameron, Kenneth, *English Place Names,* Methuen, 1961

Cook, Chris, *Macmillan Dictionary of Historical terms*, The Macmillan Press Limited, 1990

Davison, Alan and Harle, Brian, *Town Trails for Morpethians*, nos 1–10, Northumberland County Library Service, 2007 to 2011 and onward

Eyre S R, *The Curving Plough-strip and its Historical Implications,* Agricultural History Review, c1956

Fergusson, James, *Morpeth from the Accession to the Jubilee of Queen Victoria,* 1887

Finlayson, R, Hardie, C et al, *Morpeth: Northumberland Extensive Urban Survey,* Northumberland County Council, 2009

Gooch, Leo, *The Desperate Faction?* University of Hull Press, 1995

Hedley, W Percy, *Northumberland Families Vol I*, Society of Antiquaries of Newcastle upon Tyne, 1968

Hodgson, John, *A History of Morpeth*, Frank Graham facsimile, 1973. First published 1832 (Refer in particular to the annals pp115-170) 1832

Kapelle, William E, *The Norman Conquest of the North*, Croom Helm, 1979

Kelly's Post Office Directory of Northumberland and Durham, 1858, 1879, 1897, 1910, 1938

Lomas, Richard, *County of Conflict*: Northumberland from Conquest to Civil War, Tuckwell Press, 1996

Lomas, Richard, *North-East England in the Middle Ages,* John Donald, 1992

Maddison, Margaret, *email to author,* 2010

Moffatt, Frederick, *Millennium: 1000 Years of Morpeth,* self published, 2000

Moffat, F, *From Bowles Green to Bullers Green,* c2000, self published

Orwin, C S and Orwin, C S, *The Open Fields*, 3rd Edition, Oxford University Press, 1967

Pigot, *Directory for Northumberland*, 1822/1828

Rawlinson, R, *Morpeth Collectanea Vol 2, Report to the General Board of Health on a Preliminary Inquiry into the sewerage, drainage and sanitary condition of the inhabitants of the Borough of Morpeth and the village of Bedlington,* 1849

Robson, D, *Autobiography,* unpublished, 1971 -1973

Rowland, Harry, *Visit Historic Morpeth,* private print, 1986

The Times Atlas of European History, Times Books, Harper Collins, 1994

Tweddle, A H, *Town Trails for Morpethians,* nos1-10, 1980s (see Davison above)

Tyson, P, *Morpeth: :An Archaeological Study,* in Archaeology in the North: report of the Northern Archaeological Survey, 1976

Watson, Godfrey, *The Border Reivers,* Sandhill Press, 1974

Willis, Ian, *Morpeth: a Northumbrian Market Town in the Nineteenth Century*, in Northumbrian Panorama, Octavian Press, 1996

Wilson, *Handbook to Morpeth and Neighbourhood, c1884*, re-printed by Newgate Press, 1996

Documents, all from Northumberland Archives, Woodhorn

Morpeth Collectanea Vol 2   SANT/BEQ/28/1/7
- List of burgesses p35
- Ellison R and Fowler R, 1738, Survey of the River Wansbeck, p4
- Haiwarde 1604 map, cut version, p53
- Rawlinson, R, 1849, Report to the General Board of Health on a Preliminary Inquiry into the sewerage, drainage and sanitary condition of the inhabitants of the Borough of Morpeth and the village of Bedlington, p259

Morpeth Collectanea Vol 4   SANT/BEQ/28/1/5
- Plan of the Town of Morpeth from Actual Survey 1826, Woods, J,
- List of burgesses signed against child labour law, p134
- Old drover letter, p150
- Rawlinson report and Lumsden's Lane diagram, p240

Morpeth Collectanea Vol 5   SANT/BEQ/28/1/10
- Plan of the Town and Part of the Borough of Morpeth, 1852
- Hoggar and Rapier, 24" to mile, 2 feet to mile, p317
- Haiwarde, J, 1604 Survey of Morpeth Borough, uncut version, lithographed in Newcastle by M Lambert in 1844, p321
- Haiwarde, J, as above, uncut version, with later alterations, p323
- Ordnance Survey 1st Edition map of Morpeth

Local Board of Health plans
- Plan of the Town and Part of the Borough of Morpeth, 1852 Hoggar and Rapier, 120" to mile, 10 feet to mile,   NRO 5789
- Local Board of Health, 1853, House Drainage Plans, copies 120" to mile, 10 feet to mile   NRO 5445 (not 5455)
- Plan of the Borough of Morpeth in the township of the same, Hoggar and Rapier 1852, 24" to mile, 2 feet to mile   SANT/BEQ/28/1/10 p317

Finance Act 1910
- Land Valuation Map, 1910   NRO 436/64
  120" to mile, 10 feet to mile
- Valuation Books, Morpeth,   NRO 2000/72

Ordnance Survey
First edition 1860, 25" to mile   SANT/BEQ/28/1/10
Second edition 1897, 25" to mile
Third edition 1922, 25" to mile
First edition 1860, 120" to mile, 10.56 feet to mile   BMO/B39/ LXIV/13/19 and 13/24

Websites
(communities.northumberland.gov.uk/)
(wikipedia.org/wiki/Margaret_Tudor)
(www.keystothepast.info)

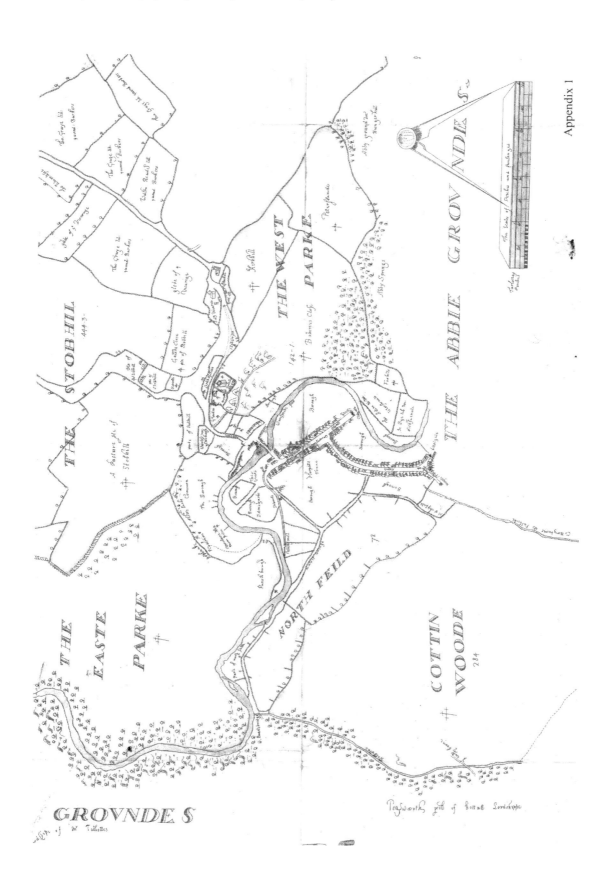

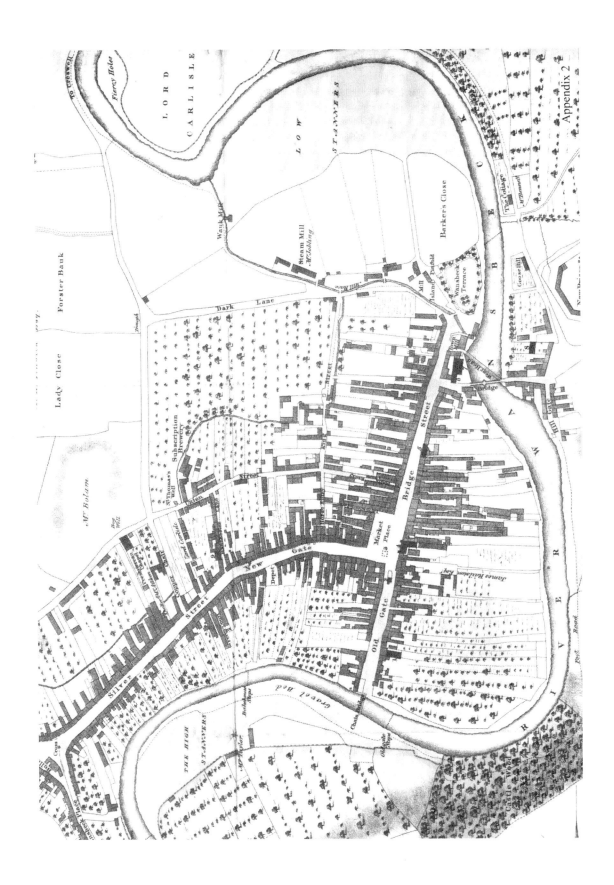

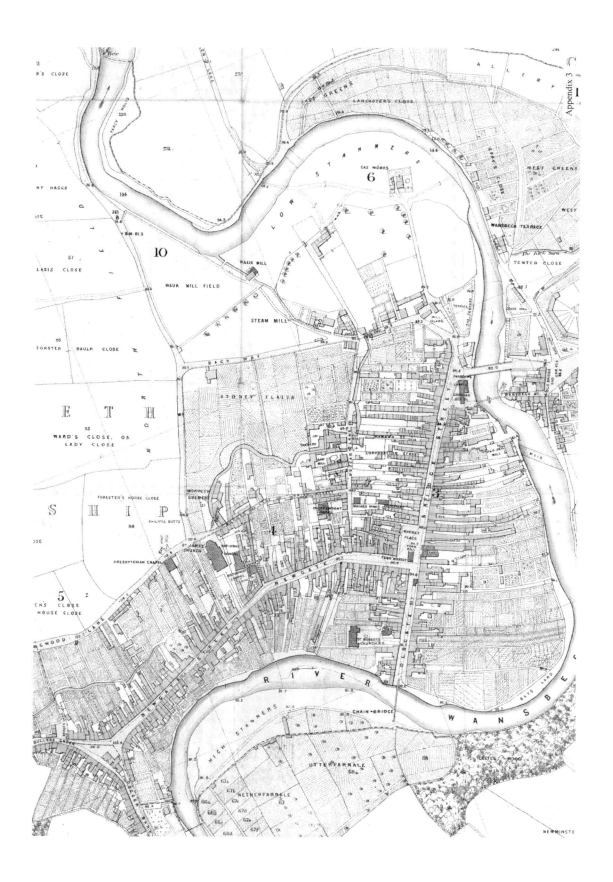

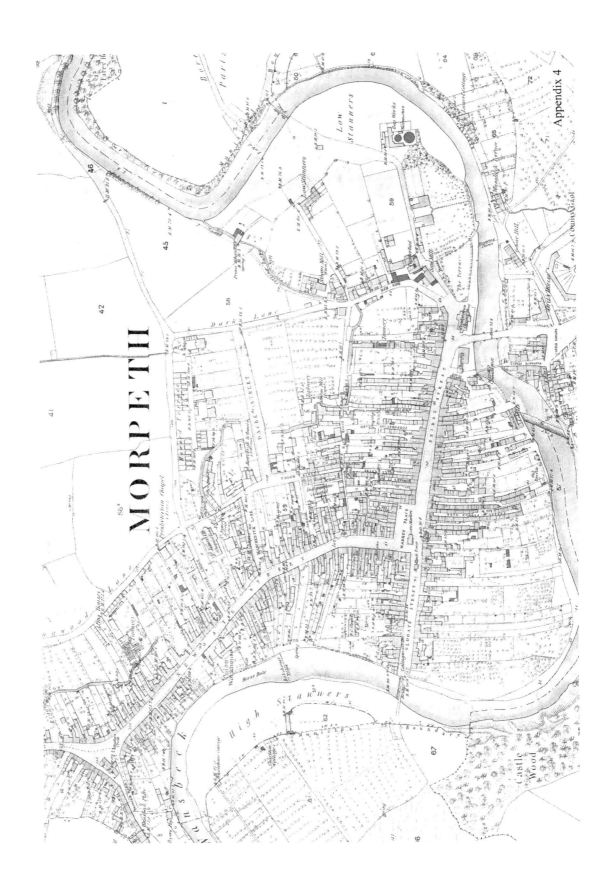

MORPETH

Appendix 5

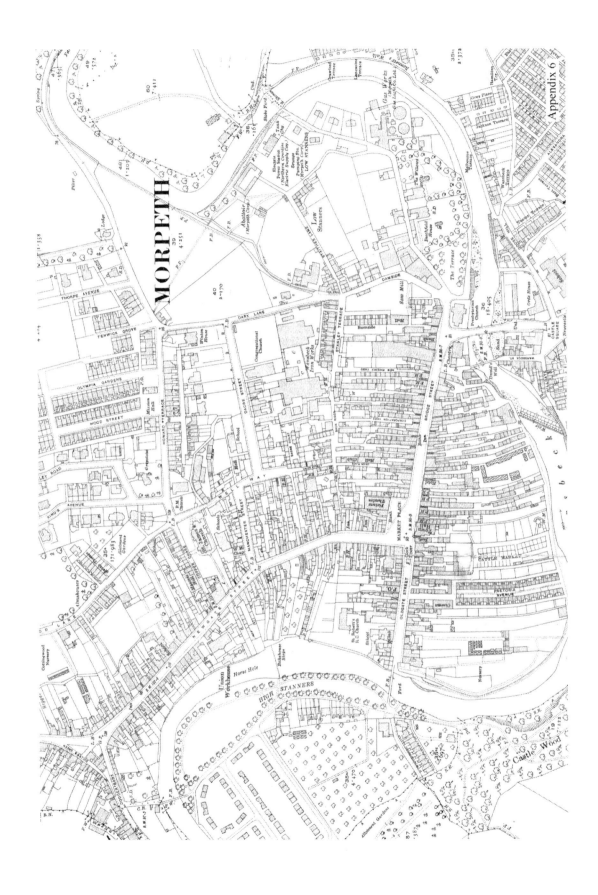

MORPETH